They Call Me Weener!

55 Short Giggle-Producing Chinwags

Trina Machacek

EMERGING
INK SOLUTIONS
Kara Scrivener, Editor
www.emergingink.com
Title Page Stock Photography: 123rf.com/illustratorovich

For Lyn
Because you and I have come so far.
Thank you!
Fly high, always.
Be happy, happy all the time.

About the Cover

    Quite by accident I took the picture you see on the cover. It was taken off my back deck one cool June morning as I was screwing around with these fuzzy pink slippers I had found hiding in the back of a closet. I gotta tell you, they have to be at least 20 years old. I bought them because they were cute, but never wore them. See, life is a wonderful journey and suddenly, in 2018, my double-occupancy journey became a single-occupancy one. But – HAHAHA a blushing-pink but – now my pink, fuzzy slippers are my traveling companions.

    Where I go, they go. When I stop, they are brought out and pictures are taken. On a corner in Winslow, Arizona, in a cotton field in Texas, under a bridge in Idaho, and – *wahoo!* – off my back deck in Nevada. You meet the coolest people when you stop to take pictures of fuzzy, pink slippers on your tootsies! In the past, the pictures have been posted and shared with my Facebook friends. Then whose who see the fuzzy slipper pictures get to virtually go traveling with me. And, oh the fun we have!

    The slippers will certainly be the star of my next book! Keep your eyes peeled for me and my pink, fuzzy feet out on the road and sometime (all fingers and toes crossed) in a new book.

    It's all about the journey.

Table of Contents

Introduction

In December of 2012, I wrote a Christmas story. I made copies and posted them around our little town to give those who stopped to read my silly story some entertainment. A week or so later, I received some very nice comments. Who knew right? Then, out of the need for validation because I am girl and full of self-doubt, I started to enlist some of my friends to read a few things and asked them to tell me what they thought – I wanted them to give it to me with both barrels and they did. To my surprise, they kinda liked what I blabbered about.

Thus, "Is This You?" was born! ITY (pronounced i-teee!) as I refer to my words, is a weekly observance that regales readers with facts that promote one main idea – we are all the same in some way. My little group of weekly readers lovingly became ITY-Inputters. I would email them a little truism in story form and they would tell me yea or nay.

Then I met Baxter Black in Elko, Nevada, a long-time participant at the annual Cowboy Poetry Gathering who was also putting on a seminar for fledgling writers. He mentioned that to get where we wide-eyed wannabes want to go with this writing stuff, we should shoot arrows of our stuff up into the sky and follow them to see just where they landed.

I had brought a few of my stories with me that day. I still don't know why. But as the seminar ended, I wrote a short note about him being my first arrow. With a lint-covered paper clip that I found in the bottom of my purse, I clipped my note to the crinkled funnies I brought and approached the cool cowboy with stars in my eyes. He was very nice and even signed my program. He's a lefty like me so I, of course, took that as a good sign. Then, I gave my spiel, asking him to read them if he ever got a chance and, if he felt like it, to let me know how bad they were. Man, oh man, was I nervous. I think I actually thrust my little makeshift portfolio at him and walk-ran to the nearest exit.

Well, what do you know? About a week later – yes, just a week later – I got the nicest letter from Baxter telling me he had read my do-dahs on the plane ride home and had liked 'em and thought they were funny. *Wow!* Maybe I *was* funny; maybe I was onto something. I mean, this guy had his own newspaper column "On the Edge of Common Sense," several books under his belt, and even had a spot on Rural TV. He told me to contact a wonderful gal in his office, Vikki Drewel, if I ever needed anything. At the end of his letter, he urged, "Go get 'em, T." So, with Baxter's arrow in my pocket, I plowed forward and never looked back.

A stitch of confidence was starting to swell inside me. I next approached Kirk Kern, the editor of our town's newspaper *The Eureka Sentinel.* To my happy surprise, I talked him into giving me and "Is This You?" a go as a weekly column. I was *way* more than excited.

Since then, "Is This You?" has grown. Not too fast, but steadily and today I have ITY-Inputters reading me in more than two but less than a ton of newspapers each week. And I thank the editors every week when they stuff my words online and in the pages of their papers.

On the pages of this book are some of my favorite columns I've written over the years. Or as I like to call them, my do-dahs. "Columns" sounds kind of snooty; do-dahs is just more *me*. I have also added a few new thought-provoking rambles that are sometimes just too long for newspapers. One do-dah – Chapter 11 – was hard to write despite it being my favorite. But it was written with love and respect. Chapter 33 came in a very close second. But that Chapter 11, that one will give you some rare insight into this writer's brain.

Seems that I am a chatty little thing. I just don't understand why an editor can't give me a whole page to go on and on and on… Silly editors!

I do hope you get your giggle on while reading these little story-like tidbits. If you wish to become an ITY-Inputter, don't hesitate to zip me a note and tell me what's on your mind. After all, once you Chapter 1, you will know me

2

Weener. Learning how and why I am Weener — well, you just can't *not* be friends after you learn the story of someone's nickname.

At the end of this book are some of the dearly loved notes I have received over the years from my amazing readers and insightful ITY-Inputters.

Dearest Reader, I hope you get your giggle on while reading these tidbits. Thanks for being here.

Be Happy, Happy All the Time.

Trina (a.k.a. Weener)

1

They Call Me Weenie!
For Goosey

When nicknames were being handed out, imagine my very oh-so-giddy, girlish happiness upon discovering that mine was Weenie. Yes, Weenie. You're just so green with envy you're not a Weenie, aren't you? Well, suck it up, Buttercup. There's only one Weenie and you're reading *her* Weenie tale! Luck, luck, lucky you! Okay, here's the whole sorted Weenie story.

I got a wild hair one day in high school and thought how fun it would be to run for some seat on the student council. To this day, I maintain that there was some beer involved in that decision – another sorted story. I got, as they say, a million of 'em.

As the campaign grew, a slogan was needed. I do believe I have my older sister to thank for the following:

Don't be a Weenie
Vote for Treenie!

Well, she *is* the one who would also call me Trina-Trina Purina Dog Chow when she was perturbed at something her innocent little sister (me) would do. Of course, everything I did was always unintentional. I girl-scout swear. Brothers and sisters are the only people who can get away with such pokes and jabs at each other and live to tell about them all.

Anyway, how lucky was I that I could now be Weenie! Oh yeah, sure, just waiting to hear, "Here comes

Weenie," had such a magical effect on my existence. Be still my heart! How excited might I get at the slightest notion that upon leaning in for a kiss with a cute guy, he might utter, "Oh Weenie!" *Not!*

As time marched on, years were added to my queendom and the reality of life, love, and growing up bloomed around me. At some point, Weenie sounded so, so… well, so weenie-like. So much so that after a few too many times of being called 'a weenie,' 'the weenie,' or 'just another weenie,' I was a very 'happy weenie' when the following happened...

Like most people, the formative years between 19 and 21 were significant. I was too old to be a silly gum-snapping giggler who had sleepovers with girlfriends, popping corn, and talking trash while looking at magazines. But I was still too young to visit the neighborhood watering hole to shoot pool and down a few brewskees. Yes, those years.

My time growing up and being an in-between-er in a little town in Eastern Nevada holds a treasure trove of memories for me. Every little town in every state will have some in-between-ers residing within that towns' boundaries. Sure, being an in-between-er in a little town had its drawbacks, but there were more events and activities I attended that have gold stars of wonder glued next to their memories rather than marks of disdain – like the weekend gatherings of a few in-between-ers… and their friends and their friends' friends and so on.

We would fit as many people as we could into my 1973 bright-yellow Pinto, a blue Ford pick-up, a Dodge Dart, a Plymouth Duster, and any other vehicle that had enough gas to get us "there" and back. Nobody I remember was ever put in charge of or took the lead as to where or when these social activities would occur. It is still a mystery as to the development of the weekend summer festivities that were held at an out-of-the-way gravel pit, lake, or campground. I credit those get-togethers for putting Weenie in my past and opening a door to countless opportunities, a door that, once I stepped through, I never looked back!

I guess I need to put in some type of a disclaimer here…

I know that drinking beer (among other things) before turning 21 was reckless and illegal. But it was what it was and although I do not condone it, I will not say the times did not happen. I often look back and get down on my knees and thank God that I made it through it all. I know of many who did not. And I am very thankful that where I grew up, it was all in fun. It was on the cusp of life-altering drugs but I, unlike some I knew and now know, did not fall into that pit. We all have pasts that we like to remember fondly even though they were not all lace and fancy tea cups. It is what it is and I still smile when I think of my in-between years. I hope you do too. Now then, back to the party, uh, story....

After a few rounds of beer had been consumed at one of those spur-of-the-moment, out-in-the-boonies beer parties, someone hollered at me across the dancing flames of the enormous bonfire. The air reverberated with the Doobie Brothers, The Stones, and Todd Rundgren from some unseen eight-track player. Yes, an eight-track player; it was the seventies!

Turning to see who had called me, I heard, "Hey Weener, send over a beer." Just like that, in a moment of beer-induced fun and frolic, magically and suddenly, I was pulled into adulthood and Weener was born! I had finally found my path. No longer would "they" have a weenie to kick around. There would be no more weenie waggin' or jabbin'. Everyone's favorite weenie was thrown into the fire and burnt to a crisp that warm, summer night.

Hey, you just can't make this stuff up.

2

Blonde in Age Only
For Donna

We've always sat in the back row at church. No real reason for this. It just happened that way. So, the back of my head has not been an issue – until now. I was drying my hair after a shower one day when I happened to see what I thought was a stray gray hair taunting me from over my shoulder. Devious little thing. I thought I would see where it came from and picked up a mirror to check out the back of my front.

Do not do this!
Do *not*, I say!

Even though my family tree graced me with brunette hair, I found that I am becoming a "blonde of age" a lot faster than what the front of my head of hair has been telling me. It won't be too much longer before I'm a palomino instead of a chestnut mare. With horror, I discovered a streak of gray on the back of my head. Immediately I stomped into the living room and announced to my other half that I was old. Old! Old, I say.

He looked up from his AARP magazine and asked how I knew I'm all of a sudden old. I turned around, pointed at the back of my head, and said, "Look, look at what is happening back there! Just look!" In a calm, comforting, loving way, he said to me with a straight face, "It's been there a while, you know."

Aarrgghh!

A hiss of air escaped me as I was deflated like one of those inflatable pumpkins or holiday Santas that adorn front yards. But plugging me back in was not going to do any good.

This is not a female-only dilemma. Oh no! This one encompasses us all at one point. Of course, that doesn't in any way make this step in life any easier to accept. It still feels like a glob of peanut butter stuck between my mouth and throat.

So, I harrumphed and mumbled my way back to the bathroom to gander at my new streak of silver lightning. Yep, it was there and the more I looked, the bigger it got. I combed and rearranged things back there, but the more I worked to not see my new mane, the more I uncovered.

I finally understand what my friend had told me while we were at a funeral some time ago. Standing behind where I sat, she had leaned over and remarked about the *few* strands of new silvery color that had showed up in my bangs. I had told her that I had earned every one of them. She had laughed and so had I, nervously. Looking back, I do believe she saw many, *many* more new, little friends up there than I was letting myself see. So, no more hiding now. No howdy!

I know – because I was there when I was born – that I am exactly blabbity-blabbity years old. I don't deny that. But I usually only feel just a stitch over *tee-hee-hee* years old. Of course, realistically, there is much you can do to cover, hide, shroud, and veil the goodies that time leaves for you to find in the mirror. But I will not let some gift on my head from Father Time take the *tee-hee-hee* outta me!

I don't believe that men age slower than ladies. I also don't believe that it is any different for men to discover that Father Time has taken a few steps across their paths either. We all have a little vanity. But the important thing is to keep it *little*.

I read a story some time ago where four grandmothers, like in there 80s, sat in a dressing room at a swimming pool talking. One noticed and remarked that gravity was indeed winning the war in respect to body parts they all had and that it was comfortable to finally just let vanity step to the side and talk to each other without the trappings of society. I think I am there with the back of my head. And the front too. Not so much with other body parts — just yet.

But I will still try to cover up my shiny friends on the back of my head with a braid or maybe swing a swirl of hair from the side and pin it there with a barrette. Oh, and I'm sure now that I will continue to sit in the back row at church!

3

Dream a Little Dream
For Sheryl

Monsters lived under my bed when I was a kid. Not in the closet, for heaven's sake; that would just be silly. Besides, there was absolutely no room left in my closet for dust bunnies, let alone monsters. No, monsters lived only under my bed. Still do to this day, on some nights. Like last night.

I will not bore you with the ugly details of the bad dream that poked me awake. Needless to say, I woke up wondering, like I did as a kid, how in the world I was going to jump all the way from my bed to the door. If I make it to the door, you see, the monster cannot grab my feet and pull me into his lair. I will be beyond his reach!

Then the fog cleared and I remembered I was a grown up and, of course, there was no monster under my bed. But – yes, a monster-sized *but* – just in case, when my feet hit the floor, I did stretch them out a bit further than usual before I stood up. It worked. He didn't get me…

So where did this fear come from? I still get chills when I recall the worst nightmare I had as a kid. In the dream, I was running through a jungle with my friend Sheryl and we were being chased by, what my brain was telling me, were head hunters. I can still feel the humidity and the huge green leaves of the jungle growth slapping at my face. The boogie men, who it turned out were head hunters with white lines painted on their faces and bone thingies in their noses, caught us and we were sat in a big old cast iron pot of steaming water. Then the boogie-woogie guys cut off our noses with – ready? – pencil sharpeners! Crazy, right? I still remember waking up in a cold sweat and sitting up, heart pounding. From the top bunk, I could see the light was still on in the hall, so I tried to call out but I was afraid if I was too loud, the headhunters would come back. So, I squeaked, "Mom, Mom?" But of course, she didn't hear me. I thought about jumping from the bed to the doorway, but it might as well have been a mile. No way could I make it. I lay there for what felt like hours, maybe even days. It was, in reality, only a few minutes before I fell back to sleep.

Waking the next morning to sunshine coming through the windows, I gingerly, slowly, fearfully raised my hand to my face and found that it had been a dream; my nose was still there. What a relief! It was quite a night since I still remember it some decades later. It must have had something to do with that game of I'm-going-to-get-your-nose-with-my-hand my grandfather used to play all in fun. Do you still do that? Well don't, it causes nightmares!

I have given this much thought over the years. Where did all that come from? Why do we have these events? Here is my unscientific, uneducated (except for that school-of-life education) thought process of why the monsters live under our beds, even as grown-ups.

Yes, sometimes the day awakens the terrors of the night. Like watching *The Wizard of Oz* and then dreaming the flying monkeys are trying to swoop down and grab you by the shirt collar to fly you off to the witch's dark, gloomy castle where you will be committed to hard labor for eternity. That, I think, is why to this day I mostly wear t-shirts – no collars for the flying monkeys to grab!

However, after many years of life, here is the ultimate reason I have come up with as to why we dream. It is how our minds flush. Yep, just like the porcelain throne.

I wonder what my neurologist friend would think of my perception.
Moving on…

Your mind carries billions upon billions of pieces of stuff that need to be expelled or dealt with. It needs to be able to start a new, with fresh batches of stuff. You go through your day zipping here and there, doing this and that, that your brain needs to, let's say, re-boot. Hence nightmares, or if you are in a particularly grand place in your life, amazing happy dreams. Some are really great dreams. Those are your brain rewards. Treasure each of them, but flush the poopie ones.

If you have the where-with-all, you could probably put some sort of recording device in your bedroom so when the pencil sharpener-carrying headhunters come for you in the night, you will be able to pick up the sound of a giant flush somewhere deep in the jungle. Sleep well.

As a side note, after I sent this to my friend who is a neurologist, he responded with a note in which he explained that yes indeed, your brain does do a nightly flush. Gee! I was just guessing. Guess I'm a pretty good guesser. His note is included in the Notes from Readers at the back of this book.

4

A Cold in Threes

For Every Man I've Ever Met

My theory of a cold is this: three days coming, three days here, and three days going. I've been living this theory for as long as I can remember. Well, for as long as it has been since I made it up, which is probably about 40 years. But it seems to be somewhat true. This is how it goes...

You wake up one morning, or in the middle of the night, or even from a quick nap, and your throat is kinda scratchy and dry. You swallow, feel pain, and think it's because your mouth is all dry and sticky – even though you do not snore or sleep with your mouth open! HAHA But you swallow and you can taste it. That taste of sick, that stale-bread-and-bad-popcorn taste and your ears might pop as you swallow. Yep, here comes a cold. Somewhere, somehow, someone breathed on you and your body opened up the gates to your nose and in came the cold virus. Swell.

From here, you can proceed in one of three ways.

You can try to shake it off, get up, take a hot shower, and pretend that you don't feel as though your feet are starting to sink into quicksand; pretend that when you look in the mirror, your eyes do not look like what my mother would call "Two pee holes in the snow."

Or...

You can let the cold overtake you, fall into bed like a wet noodle, and slither under the covers hoping that the next time you wake up, it was all a dream...

Or you can do what most adults do – just live with it!

"Just living with it" needs to have a plan of action for the next three days (which will *not* be the worst three days), the three days you're actually sick (which *will* be the worst three days), and then the last three days that drag by like they are three weeks long.

Let me help you out here and give you my contingency plan. So, the first three days…

Gather supplies. When you are sick, you get to be sick. That entails having the expensive orange juice, the one that you usually only get during the holidays when your Great-Aunt Sadie is visiting. You also get to buy the softest nose tissues with aloe, even though they can't be used to clean your glasses because they smear the glass with aloe.

During your sick time, you get to drink really great tea from a box that doesn't have 250 bags in it for $3.50. You also should get the remote. But there may be some blowback from that as you should be in bed, not in the living room spreading your germs from you to every surface you touch.

Supplies laid in, wait to develop into a full-blown, flu-like cold. The second three days, you don't care about the orange juice. You never want another cup of tea because you are exhausted from getting up every 15 minutes to get rid of it! And of course, you have decided that even though you get, like, 578 channels, there is nothing on television worth watching…

This sounds all too familiar, doesn't it?

Well, your nose is now as red as a cherry tomato and your pajamas need to be changed – really change your pajamas after a few days, *please!* You have just about decided you are going to go to the doctor because you know that a shot in the rear end and some "real" medicine, not the stuff from over the counter, is the only thing that will save you.

But you know – because, after all, you are an adult – that what the doctors, the nurses, the pharmacist at your local drug store, and your neighbor has told you and your spouse, your mother, and your sister that a cold will not respond to antibiotics, no matter what your Great-Aunt Sadie has told you in the past as you visualize her downing that cool refreshing last swallow of the good orange juice you bought because you are sick.

But just as you feel you will call to see if you can get in to see a medical professional, something amazing happens. It is day six and a half. You are moving into the last three days and you feel a tiny bit better. You are a tiny bit hungry. Not double-cheeseburger-hungry, but maybe a tuna-sandwich-with-a-pickle-hungry. You take a bite and, low and behold, you can *taste* it! Ta-da!

Moving into the last three days of this cold, you are not out of the woods yet. You still have to go through the dry stuffiness stage. You can still feel *it* in your nose, but you can't coax it out with any amount of blowing. Your sinuses are dry, you are coughing and hacking, and you just can't get that desired full breath of air.

Then as a last parting shot at that stinking cold, a final "see you 'round buddy," what do you do to get back in your groove? Well, you finish it off with that perfect orange juice – straight from the carton while standing at the refrigerator with the door open – and you realize that indeed, you have won the battle.

You are – A True Survivor.

5

Downsize to Who?

For Dennis

One fine, spring day, when I was 14, I got my first real paycheck after cleaning tables in the lunchroom at the high school I went to. I see 14-year-old children now and I don't remember being as grown up as they are. I was just a geeky kid with a $33-paycheck burning a flame-driven hole in my pocket. Thirty-three dollars is *still* a stack to me, but to some, thirty-three dollars is no more than one trip through the local you-want-fries-with-that? lane of the drive thru.

I know today that some checks are never cashed just because they are not worth the time of the payee. I have written small payroll checks for under, say, $70 that were never cashed. That is amazing to me. You work, you get paid, and you don't cash the check because it isn't worth your time? But I'm spinning the wrong way…

That $33 payday is etched in my pea-picking brain. I can still see the check in my hands. It was the first all-printed check with my name on it that I had ever received – not cash from my parents for doing chores, although that was always accepted by my greedy little, sticky hands. Not cash for babysitting. I hated babysitting, but I liked money. That check was a *real* paycheck that had to be cashed – at a bank – by me! Man, I couldn't cash it and spend it fast enough.

Wondering what I bought? Well, since I remember it like it was only 40-plus years ago, I'll tell you. I bought a Slinky. Yes, a Slinky. A shiny, wiggly, made-that-slinky-music-when-you-bobbled-it-from-hand-to-hand Slinky. I had wanted one for some time and had thought about buying it from the first day I went to work washing tables, clearing litter, moving garbage cans, and smelling the leftover lunch after everyone was gone. Ah, memories in living smell-o-vision!

Yes, I know that a Slinky isn't like buying a book, a collectable clock, or a piece of jewelry to have and to hold forever. All that grown up stuff came later as I was, well, growing up. That fine spring day, it was all about the Slinky. And I'm guessing it lasted all of about three whole days until that slinking spring toy got all matted up within itself and ended up in a ball of silvery frustration in one of those cafeteria garbage cans. Yes, the life of a Slinky, just going down, down, down stairs – never up. Never gave that a thought, did you?

I didn't learn from that buyer's choice decision. Didn't learn to buy better, to think of the future, to plan with money. I, it seems, have a tendency to just blow and go. Money runs through my hands like water through a sieve. No 401k has followed me through life. No IRA awaits me turning some special age. And since my other half and I have always worked for ourselves, it is a good thing that I was paired up with someone who bought his first hammer at the tender age of, like, four. That same little hammer is still in his toolbox – that and mountains of so many other life purchases. Ah. Now we are getting somewhere. What to do with stuff when the buying time finally passes, if it ever does!

One of the newer watchwords for those getting ready and sliding to retirement is *downsizing*. That is where I currently find myself. Downsizing. But for such a simple word, just ten little letters, (you went back and counted the letters, didn't you? HAHA) it has implications that encompass a lifetime of picking up this and that. Not big things, not expensive things, not life-altering things worth tons of moolah. Just the Slinkys of life. What to do with all that stuff?

I am coming to the realization that the world today is not the world of our yesterday. There are not too many four-year-olds who know what a hammer is, let alone buy one and keep it for, like, the next 65 years with an anvil, pliers, and tractor… But there are a few. Yes, there are! We just need to find them. Those younger than me that are just itching to get nostalgia-ized.

I must admit that occasionally I am a woman of the world – the world of no patience. Wanting it all done and done now. Things sometimes move only as fast as a sloth in my lane while the world zings along like a rabbit racing to get the carrot that is actually tied on a string attached to a stick being held over his head by a guy who is paid to do it and only does it because he needs to grow his 401k in the lane next to me. *Whew*. Dang me, there's another reference to that elusive 401k that I have never had an opportunity to have and grow and… Oops, my green-eyed monster is showing and glowing…

Rabbit it along, Trina!

Rational realization has slowly sunken into my gray matter. All the treasures we have accumulated were treasures someone before us had accumulated and when our paths crossed, they were at the downsizing point of their lives. We were the sloths and they were the rabbits. Now, I am on the biggest hunt of all – finding the next home for all things lovingly picked up and placed on shelves to be enjoyed and dusted and looked at occasionally and dusted and dusted and, well, you get the idea.

I need to find the next "me" for all my stuff. Things make the rounds, from one treasure hunter to the next. Do you suppose that is why the world is round? Oh, Columbus had no idea!

6

Duck! Rudeness Alert
For Darlene

Sometimes I finish my other half's sentences. But *only* when I know what he is trying to say. Then *only* when I feel he is grasping for words. Oh, and occasionally when we are talking to each other or to someone else. I even "help" him finish lines when he is on the phone. Then there are the times he is reading aloud from a magazine or a book and I chime in, ending a sentence, even if I don't know the end of the sentence he is reading.

Well, seeing all the finish lines I cross for him all gathered up like that, I seem to talk for him a lot, huh? Now that I can see in black and white my self-imposed helpfulness, I think this behavior is rude. Which makes me a rude, little dickens. Rude.

Now there's a strange-sounding word. **Rude.**

Rude.

Rude. Nope, no matter how many times you say it, it sounds, well, *rude.*

Just how far do you have to push the envelope before you become rude? Is it rude to blow your nose at the table? Depends on if you use a tissue or not! Yuck! I don't think we should pursue this line of conversation. It would be rude – and gross. *Especially* gross.

Isn't it still rude to put your hand in someone's face as they are talking to you? Or talking over someone as they are talking? This last one I saw on television recently. Of course, the people involved were major politicians, so I guess they figure they are allowed to be as rude as possible. Not to be outdone by those two bigwigs, it seems like news commentators and talking heads also speak over one other.

How do I decipher what is actually going on in the country when everyone talks at the same time? So, you know what I did? I put my hand up in front of the television, said, "Talk to the hand," and then stuck my nose in a book. Felt just wonderful.

There are so many ways to be rude that I had a time picking and choosing which ones to focus on. Besides interrupting and that nose-blowing situation, how about staring, ignoring, picking teeth, snapping gum in church, and cutting in line? Oh, there are many more rude behaviors that are just *not* talked about.

What is one of the first rude behaviors we learn not to do? Pointing. We start as small fries, pointing at things and people that are not what we usually see. Kids are very susceptible to pointing. And mothers are quick to grab those tiny, sticky hands, smiling as the object of "the point" looks back with either a knowing smile or a grimace angrily directed at a child who knows no better. "It's not polite to point," the mother will say – but she usually will follow up by staring at what the tike was pointing at because she can't believe that anyone would go to the store dressed like a smurf and stand in the cereal aisle! Weird.

There are degrees of pointing. As an adult, I don't point with my finger, I point with my eyes or my head. We were recently in a store and I saw a young guy in the electronics department who was about six-foot-six-inches tall which, by itself, isn't all that uncommon. However, he had a bright-orange Mohawk that added another 14 inches to his height. It wasn't just on the top of his head. Oh no! It was from his forehead all the way down to the nape of his neck. Looked kind of like a sun burst from the side.

Of course, I didn't want my other half to miss the scenic view so I pointed – with my head. Must have looked like a bobble head going *bouncity boink*, like I had some sort of tick that caused my head to bounce from upright to my left shoulder. Internally, I shouted, *Look! Look!*

Other times, we point with just our eyes. Pointing with your eyes is a bit more subtle than head pointing. It isn't eye rolling, which is pointing and communicating something like, "Oh brother!" at the same time. Eye pointing is like head bouncing – with your eyes. Do it a bit too vigorously and you could get eye strain. In eye pointing, you try to get your cohort to look at something strange by moving your eyes quickly over and over again in the direction of what you see. Usually your eyebrows will go in unison with the eye point in the direction of what you are pointing at, but should not be pointing at, because pointing is rude.

You tried eye pointing just now, didn't you?

I did too! For practice.

7

Flying Spiders
For Dale

We find ourselves transitioning into another season. It's nearly fall, autumn, post-summer, pre-winter. So many things happen this time of year. Not that there are more or less things happening as compared to spring, but *different* things. Like watching the leaves turn on the trees. Leaf peepers are out and about, especially on the eastern seaboard.

Happily, in Nevada up in the mountains as the freezing temperatures creep from the summits down to the lowlands, the leaves on the Aspen trees, also known as Quakies, begin to change. They're called Quakies because when the wind or even a cool mountain breeze blows the leaves of these wonderful trees, they quake and shutter making the most wonderful clickity sound that urges you to lie back in the sun on a bed of summer grass and drift away... Right up until you realize you are using a cow pie for a pillow and the ground is a hot bed of ants and ticks! Yes, poets get you all fuzzy and happy and everyone has a good time until the bugs and snakes come out. *Yikers!*

Now, where was I? Oh, the Quakies. The leaves of the Quakies in the fall change from summer-green to golden-yellows, oranges, and reds, giving a grand show for anyone who is lucky enough to see them. But there is more to fall than leaves.

There is a mass movement that I'm betting most have not seen. And, if by chance you have noticed this happening, you might not guess what you were actually seeing. As spring comes and goes and summer moves along, all things in nature do the natural thing – have families. Yes, it is not just the screaming cats in the alley that interrupt your sleep. It's also the dogs and rabbits and horses and cows and spiders. Creepy-crawly spiders.

I must say here that I do not like spiders. Spiders and I have never been BFFs. All things considered we never will. So that makes this story all the more creepy – or creepier.

Warning: If you are really paranoid of spiders, you might not want to continue reading as once you learn the following knowledge, you can't un-know it and you will always be aware of what happens with spiders in the fall.

Okay, spiders spin webs; we all know that. And in those webs, they catch bugs and sometimes wrap those morsels of yumminess up in spider-web stuff to save them to snack on later. Oh, how delightful. But there is another use for those webs. It is a way for the baby spiders to go out into the world and start their own families. And here is how that is done. Well, maybe not *exactly* how it is done as I am not an entomologist, just a gal that learned about flying spiders.

One of the first signs of fall outside can be seen early in the morning along the tops of the blades of grass on your lawn. Glittering in the morning sun you can see very fine spider webs that overnight spiders have spun. It kind of looks like a shimmering sea of tiny zip lines built for tiny spiders. Quite amazing really. But then, as the days get cooler, things ramp up another notch and the baby spiders are kicked out of their spider homes and sent off. How they move is remarkable – but creepy.

They fly on webs. Yes, they do. On a warm fall day, if you are lucky enough to time it just right, you can see this mass movement. You can go outside and look up toward the sun. But not directly at the sun as you can melt your eyes. Not a good look for any of us. But turn your face kind of up toward the sun, covering the orb with your hand, and then just watch.

Occasionally you might see a shimmering trail or a glob of web flying through the air. You will think, "Wow, kinda pretty." You might see one or two, but as you watch, you will see more and more of them. Some will be really high and some you can grab out of the air. But don't grab them because there are tiny little spiders attached to those webs, flying to their new homes to create new lives and families. They fly, uh, coach not first-class, until the web catches on a tree, fence post, car antenna, clothes line, or you! I bet you have at some time or another seen a web blowing in the wind caught on something. Now you know how and why they got there. Cool, huh? But still – creepy.

So, go out and enjoy fall and all it has to offer. Cider, hunting, raking leaves, migrating geese, and the mass movement of tiny baby spiders. That should keep you up at night.

See?

Warned you!

8

Friendly Fact-Finding
For Bob

Is there a real line that needs to stay wide, bold, and un-crossable when you meet a new friend? I'm not talking about just manners. Manners should be upheld no matter where you are in a relationship – like not picking at anything that might be bothering you because it is protruding from or hiding in an orifice on your person. (Quite a visual, huh?) Or adjusting your gaze and non-apologetically looking around like there must be something better happening in another corner of the room. No, in my opinion manners are a given.

I'm more interested in how many questions and what kind of questions you can ask a new acquaintance. In most instances, I encourage the ask-away-without-abandon strategy. I mean, of course, let's not go overboard and ask things about weights and measurements. We are not working for the governmental department of statistics or taking a census. But stuff that you might want to know about a new presence in your life is, to me, fair game. Oh, and if you are asked something out of bounds, don't pussyfoot around it, just giggle and say, "Wouldn't you like to know?"

"Bite me" is also acceptable.

Just the other day, I met a few of what I now call new friends. We had a very nice chitchat. I am just a chitty-chatty kinda gal. Just start my chitty and I will continue chatty-ing like there is no tomorrow. Anyway…

I now know that one has been married for over 50 years and the other has never been married even though this new friend is probably around 70. I would not have known that if I hadn't asked. But I didn't consider it being nosey; I just wanted to know why this new friend said they were single. I thought it only natural to ask why. I was ready to talk about the death of a loved one. Or go on to ask more questions about divorce. But to my amazement, neither of these scenarios fit the bill. I had met someone who has been single throughout adulthood, even though there had been a few close calls along the way – I know that because I asked. Oh, I am here to tell you that I wanted to ask, like, a mountain-more questions about lifelong singledom, but my manners kicked in and the subject matter moved to other good conversation.

So, friendly fact-finding is fun. Just when you think you know all there is to know about someone close to you, a new factoid will reveal itself. My other half and I have been what some have said attached-at-the-hip for a long, long time. I was going to put three "longs" there but that seemed to be a bit of overkill. Just know that that third "long" was right on the tips of my fingers, scratching at the keyboard. Let's three-leg it along.

Get it?

Attached at the hip, three legged. Oh goodie, yet another interesting visual.

After over 40 years of wedded bliss – wink, wink – you would think that we would have reached the full mark on knowing everything about each other long ago. But once, and rather off handedly, I let it slide that I felt there was a very slim chance, that I might think that it was quite possible to use too much garlic in some of the wonderful dishes he created with love and, uh, garlic.

Well, you would have thought I had single-handedly sunk the Titanic since after my statement, it felt as though a *huge* iceberg had come floating through our kitchen. I said that it really was possible to add too much garlic to a dish being concocted that it could peel off the roof of your mouth.

Yeah, in retrospect that might have been a teensy bit much… I admit, I should not have said it while gobbling down some of his wonderful potato-kale soup. But to his credit (and mine), his soup is now made with just a hint of garlic and is truly amazing. So, see? You learn something new about someone even after a long, long – *a-hem* – long time.

Apparently, I do not have a very large filter in my soul. That is, if there is a filter at all. That filter, or lack thereof, is what makes me *me* and you *you*. I look forward to meeting and sharing with people.

Remember that if you want to know something about someone, for goodness sake, go to the horse's mouth. If you take the chance to find out something about someone by asking someone else? Just figure you are talking to the other end of the horse.

Happy friendly fact-finding!

9

It's Called a What?

For Jerry J.

For some 40 years, I have called the space along the road where the weeds grow unobstructed then die and collect, where the litter gathers and the water stands, where the road-killed animals tumble to a stop and the stalled cars park, *the bar pit*.

That is what my delicate girl ears heard it called when I moved to the country. That is what I still hear it called and that is what I will continue to call it. However, recently, I was given the correct terminology for that strip of real estate actually is. But before I relay to you what and why it is what it is, here are some other misnomers.

What is the difference between a flapjack and a pancake? Well, in my line of thinking, a flapjack is cooked over an open fire while camping while a pancake is made at home in the comfort of a kitchen with running water. I enjoy a flapjack with all the camping activities that go along with the outdoors – fun and frolic, campfires and getting dirty, bugs and laughing… But I also revel in eating a pancake on Sunday morning in my jammies with the only fire around being the one in the wood stove keeping me warm and cozy.

How about this? Is it called ice melt or ice melter? Since it is February as I write this do-dah, this ice melt or melter stuff is on nearly everyone's mind. Well, I say it's called ice melter as I use it to melt the slippery leg-breaking, frozen winter that at this time of the year acts like it will never recede. *Aarrgghh!* If I do not want to come crashing down with my feet pointed up to the sky, I use ice melter. It sounds funny to me to say I use ice melt. Ice melts when I use ice melter. Am I wrong?

Whoa, then there are the highfalutin food discussions. This one is just for fun rather than a real which-way-you-call-it debate. Is it goose-liver pâté or is it you-want-me-to-eat-what-on-a-cracker? The second is what I remember calling it the one and only time I was at a gathering at which the goose was cooked, uh, so to speak. So, take a big swig of Diet Coke and clean the pâté on your plate off your palate and lets' move on…

So, about this bar pit situation. I was given a class in the true name and reason for the bar pit while, again, we were on a road trip. Seems that what I know as a bar pit is actually a borrow pit. Well, that sounds weird to me. I heard *barrow*, not *borrow*. Barrow can only go with wheel – as in wheel barrow. This is getting way too deep.

Okay, a borrow pit. Why? Here is the story I was told and I'm sticking to it. In the long ago when the railroads were being built, the builder needed to designate areas to create the base or railbed on to make the railroad kinda level and not all up and down and the like. To build that railbed base-thingy, they needed to drag dirt up to make the mounds of rail bedding. Not wanting to bring dirt and rock from any distance away, the place alongside the railbed became the place they borrowed dirt from. So, from both sides of the railbed, the railroad builders created a pit from which they borrowed dirt and that pit was to remain there forever and be called a *borrow pit*. Ta-da.

Now, if you want to call it a barrow pit, you would, of course, refer to the amount of material collected from the borrow pit as a barrow, which happens to be the amount of material that a wheel barrow holds.

Oh, and yes that same theory crosses over to road building, making what I can now call a barrow, borrowing, bar pit.

Confused yet? Well, you try explaining all that with just words? It is much clearer with a ton of hand gestures. Using all your fingers! Not just that exclamation point finger.

29

10

Hobby or Sport?

For Damon

Is fishing a hobby or a sport? It depends on who is doing the fishing and why. The Montana fishermen, the ones who grab a pole, a shovel to dig worms, and a tin can to keep them in, now *those* are fishermen.

My husband really likes to fish. I like to fish too, but my attention span is that of a hummingbird. I flit – flit from one spot to the next, changing the orange lure to the pretty red one, using worms or any other matter of bait or sharp, barbed goody I can find in the tackle box. Then, about ten minutes later, my attention turns to a book or a bird bobble-heading along the water's edge. While I flit and scurry and generally never sit still long enough to catch a cold, my husband fishes with patience and calmness. I love to watch a man fish. It is like art in motion. *Sigh.*

Of course, he likes to catch too, but just the fact that he is fishing seems to be almost as good as catching. He likes to throw most of the fish back into the water, making him a catch-and-release fisherman, but he does keep enough for breakfast – which is where I come in. Yes, of course it is still all about me. HAHA.

I learned along the way by watching him how to do the after-fishing business. One day, it happened; he got sick and it became necessary for me to clean and scale the fish that were to become our breakfast. There the two trout were, lying on the picnic table still hanging on the chain-thingy (that is where you put your caught fish so they can't get away) and there I was with the water, wash pan, and knife. Oh goodie, goodie gumdrops.

First, scaling. I know there is controversy as to whether fish need to be scaled before cooking, but I am very grateful that my other half always scales the fish we devour. It just seems cleaner and you are not picking scales out of your teeth for days afterwards. *Ick.*

Fish are slippery, even in rigor. The wetter you get them to clean them, the slipperier they become. The slippery stuff gets on your hands and during the cleaning and scaling process, it just gets everywhere – arms, face, hair, pants, shirt, and the dog. This, I delightfully found, is why fishermen smell like fish at the end of the day. It isn't because they are fishing by the water. It is because the cleaning event deposits fishy stuff *everywhere.*

A deep breath and I grabbed fish number one by the tail and began the scaling process. The scales came off fairly easily as I flung them across the picnic table, leaving the fish smooth to the touch. I continued; scale, fling, wipe knife on pants – scale, fling, wipe knife on pants. After years of watching him do this task with ease and finesse, I'm sure my first attempt made our camp look like a massacre had occurred.

Then, skipping the gory details, let's just say I got the stuff from the inside of the fish to the outside of the fish and disposed of it without too much trouble. I'm more than sure I could not do that to a deer or other large trophy-sized animal. I'm glad though that there are those who can because I like to eat. Just a bit of commentary…

Eventually both fish were emptied of their innards, stripped naked of scales and fins and (*gulp*) their heads were removed with a crunch of knife to bone. A final wash with clean water and the two fish were bagged and put away to become breakfast the next morning. Which they were. Yummy.

So, is fishing a hobby or a sport? I thought for a while and decided that after getting all the gear together, driving to the fishing hole, setting camp, going through the tackle box, readying the poles, getting to the water, catching, cleaning, cooking, and re-cleaning afterwards, it sounds like work – feels kinda like work too. But the sigh and smile you hear and see around the campfire after a good day of fishing makes me say, fishing is neither a hobby nor a sport. It is a lifestyle.

11

Lost and Found

For Jerry

On January 11, 2018, my other half passed away. So, this little Number-11 do-dah was done just for him. It ran in newspapers the week after his departure. Oh, it was hard, but it was as they say – whoever *they* are – a true labor of love. ITY Inputters across the country let me know I was loved and that I had hit the mark with this goodbye. Now, don't sniffle. He is still in many ways telling me what's-what! Enjoy.

Yesterday, January 11th, my husband, my other half of nearly 42 years, passed away. Now, I tell you this not so you'll be sad for me – although I *am* sad enough for me, you, and anyone else you can see, hear, or think of – but to rejoice in the knowledge that he is now in a wonderful place. And since over the years "Is This You?" has typically been a giggle-fest, you probably already know that I will keep this light, even though it deals with the death of my loved one...

When someone is gone forever from your life, it is referred to as a loss. But it is not like the loss of that one sock somewhere in the washing machine. I have thought of this for the past week. He isn't *lost*. I know exactly where he is and I rejoice in knowing that.

Really, I figure it's called a loss because there is no other word for it. I mean, if you check out a thesaurus under "loss" you can find alternatives. But you wouldn't say, "Sorry for your deficit" or "Sorry for your defeat." I think, at this time, I should like to think that I am just sorry to be alone.

So, as irreverent as you may see it, here are some "tales out of school" that I have used to keep my sanity and to keep the faces of those around me from looking at me with such fear that they will say the wrong thing – because, as I see it, there is no "wrong" thing to say when you are trying to comfort a soul who is now alone.

We entered the hospital and, after a few days, found that it was a real possibility I would be leaving alone. In fact, during that time my other half had a very good friend of 60-plus years in another hospital fighting for his life at that moment. We talked about how strange it was that the two of them had gone through so much together over the years. Their biggest pastime had been building cars and when they were young, driving fast and racing – a lot.

So, in my special way, to keep things light, I asked my other half what he thought he was doing being sick. Were he and his friend racing to the grave? He laughed. His friend was not out of the woods, but he was still fighting the good fight. So, ta-da! Look at who won that race!

At one point, my other half experienced some hallucinations. While looking out the window, he called to me, "Look at the Eskimos outside on the roof!" It lasted for just a few seconds, then the confusion was gone and he knew there were no Eskimos outside on the roof. So, I asked him if he knew where the Eskimos went. He knew what was coming, laughed, shook his head, and recited this little poem I had made up about squirrels that we used over the years. But he put in Eskimos instead of squirrels.

"The Eskimos were in their little Eskimo houses in their little Eskimo beds and had pulled their little Eskimo blankets up over their little Eskimo heads."

So even though we kinda knew that we, well, *he* was fighting what we Christians call the last fight, he was still a funny guy and he was using my line doing it!

Over the years, we had discussed our mortality numerous times and decided that we would both be cremated at the end of our time on Mother Earth. Off-handedly, you say you will be cremated and it slides off your shoulder like melting butter. But in my mind, and maybe yours too, you get to wondering, *What if there is just a hint of life in me when the oven goes whoosh?*

At the mortuary after all was said and done, I stayed behind to talk to the gentleman who had helped me through this last door of the process. I looked him in the eye and said without flinching, "Now, you be sure he is really gone before you light that torch, okay?"

Oh my stars, you could have heard a coffin drop!

I know – really, really know – that I heard my other half laugh. It was at that moment that even though I have, am, and will forever be a bit lost, my other half found Glory, Home, and Peace.

Oh, and he is fishing all the time! What else could I want for him?

The following is posted on the mirror in his bathroom. It is surrounded by a picture of the wild rose bush he planted for me years ago. I look forward to seeing it bloom every year.

The Deepest Level of Worship
Is Praising God, In Spite of the Pain
Thanking God during the Trials
Trusting Him when we are tempted
To lose Hope and Loving Him when
He seems so distant and far away.

At My darkest God is my Light.
At My Weakest God is my Strength.
At My Saddest God is my Comforter.

12

A Deal Is A Deal
For Bernice

I remember a time when a handshake was as good, if not better, than a 1,000-page contract. Shake a hand on a deal and that was it. No lawyers, signatures, witnesses, or notary. Just a clasp of strong hands across a table or bar and the deal was done. That was how my very favorite deal was sealed over 40 years ago – with a hand shake.

Before you learn of that deal, let's look at some remarkable deals that you may have come across in your life. Remember swearing to yourself to always be true and faithful to that one special person in school you had that fiery crush on if they would just give you a chance, look your way, or ask you to, or say yes to your shaky invite to the dance? That was such a huge deal you made with yourself. Did it last?

How about the deal with your parents to always be a safe and sane driver, and keep the car clean and full of gas if they let you take it out Saturday night? Parents are sometimes such easy marks. Did you keep your end of that deal? Oh please, we were teenagers!

You can get into the diet deals too. I have certainly done that. These deals include: not having the cookie so the pants will fit better next week and eating my veggies instead of the cake so I can finally see my toes. Well, I still wear the same size pants and my toes look the same as they always have. I bet over my years, I have lost and regained and lost again enough weight that would be the equivalent of three small children, a puppy, and maybe even a set of four new tires mounted on 16-inch five-hole Ford truck rims.

I've only just recently come to the realization that my German heritage has instilled in me a largeness I am unable to escape after more years of numbers on my scale going up and down than I can shake a stick at – whatever that means. Really. Okay, maybe. I am such a girl.

It's just a number. I do try to keep healthy. It keeps my doctor happy. A happy doctor on your side is like always having 20 dollars in your pocket – you might not always need it, but it's better to have it than not.

I surmise we have all, at one time or another, made a deal with our God for some amazing wants and wishes. I wasn't ready for my mom to die and I told Him that. That was when I found out that sometimes His answer is, "No." *Dang it!* But after some reflection, I finally realized that from my side, the answer appeared to be "No," but from my mom's side, it was "Yes." Her pain was gone and she had been rewarded with glory. It's all in how you look at it.

Ah, now to reward you for your patience. Here are the facts of my deal of a lifetime.

When my husband proposed marriage, I, of course, blushingly agreed. He had no idea what he was in for. It has been some ride. But the two things we shook hands on, the deal we made that day, the two things that were as important to us then as they are now are as follows:

My promise to him – to always put the toilet paper on the roller-thingy so it rolls from the top.

His promise to me – to never complain that I squeeze the toothpaste tube from the middle.

The rest was just gravy. Sometimes all smooth and creamy and sometimes chunky and lumpy. What's the deal of your lifetime?

Okay, so while we are here, let's just touch on the toilet paper debate. Yes, I am in the paper-comes-from-the-top camp. I know people who are trying to live in the paper-comes-from-the-bottom-camp and they are, of course, *wrong.* To let them know just how wrong they are, I unapologetically change the toilet paper in their bathrooms when I visit.

By marriage, I got Aunt Bernice whom I loved dearly but who was laughingly in the aforementioned wrong camp. So, when we visited her, I changed her TP for years and years and we giggled and laughed because she would change all the rolls in my house too. I have no shame in many areas of my life and this one is a big number one – even when it is number two.

Am I alone in this?
No.

Is it an important life-altering thing?
No, of course not.

But the most important thing concerning this never-ending toilet paper debate is that I, of course, am right!

Hey, it's just the way I…

Wait for it –

Roll!

13

Are you *kidding* me?
No way no how am I going to tempt the fates by putting in a

13!

Now, go throw salt over your left shoulder…
While standing on your right foot and be sure you are facing to the West.

Whew, that was close.

Let's move on.

Quickly, people.
Quickly!

HAHAHAHAHAHA

14

A Yawn Starter
For Claude

A yawn, I have learned from a neurologist friend, starts in the brain. Something somewhere in there is triggered and through a pathway unknown to this plain, regular human, it makes you urgently suck in air and disturb the silence with that yawn *aarrgh* sound. Sometimes you close your eyes or your head may sway like a palm tree in the hot desert wind as you inhale. Then, after getting as much air as possible into your lungs and making a sound that could possibly match a soprano's exalted eight-octave C, we exhale with calmness and a sense of completion. You just can't get that feeling of accomplishment any cheaper anywhere.

Sometimes it's nearly impossible to pay strict attention to a conversation. Even if the topic *is* really interesting. Like space travel. I like listening about space travel. Well, not so much listen to someone go on and on about space travel as much as I like to look at outer space pictures, like the ones taken by the Hubble telescope. Now, if someone was talking about those cool Hubble pictures and they were showing stuff about outer space, now that would capture my attention. But even when the topic is fun, interesting, amusing, or important, a yawn will emerge from somewhere deep inside your brain.

In my family there have been some wonderful yawners. My father could wake an entire neighborhood with that first ground-quaking yawn in the morning. I'm pretty sure if yawning was an Olympic event, he would have won a metal in it.

Sometimes I find myself yawning at the most inappropriate times. You know, when someone is talking to you, usually close and face-to-face. All of a sudden, you feel a yawn developing – wherever yawns begin developing. You feel it... and here it comes, that urge to suck in air through your nose and mouth. Try as you might, you just can't stop it once it makes its way into your consciousness. You might try to stifle it by covering and trying to keep your mouth shut, but that just makes you get all squished face and your lower jaw to unhinge in an otherworldly attempt to force air into your lungs. Stifling a yawn is a lost cause, at best.

Yawing is contagious too. There are places that you can actually cause a domino effect – if you so desire. Like in church. It's kinda quiet, warm, and close quarters. Now, I know that you wouldn't do this just to see what happens. But we all know someone who would. Starting a yawn-fest is an interesting feat of human nature. Unobtrusively but not unnoticed, one will yawn with just the right amount of noise to get the attention of a few others. A little stretch and maybe a light body shiver will accompany it. Somewhat magically, another person will yawn and another then maybe, if all goes just right, even the guy behind the pulpit will get the urge and do one of the stifled yawns.

Please don't really try this. I don't need *Him* mad at me for any reason whatsoever!

Yawns come and go. But sometimes they create what I call a *yawn swarm*. This happens to me usually in the mornings. I yawn when I get up and find myself yawning over and over again even though I got enough sleep. This leads me to believe yawing doesn't have much to do with being tired. So, then why would we yawn? There is more than one scientific reason touted by professionals who have all those important letters behind their names, like PhD, MD, and PASPTTY (Pay Attention Smart Person Talking to You). Gotta put that on a t-shirt!

Those professionals will, I am sure, make us yawn when they drone on as to why we yawn. Some say it is a way our bodies try to cool down our brains while some argue it is a way for our brains to wake up the rest of our bodies. I say we yawn because, if you stop and really think about it, a yawn is kinda fun; it feels good and it's free with no strings attached! And who doesn't like free with no strings attached?

I think the only thing that might be as good of a feeling or as satisfying as a big ole yawn is a brain-clearing sneeze!

So, as you sit there – wherever you are sitting – give yourself the gift of a yawn. Cool down your brain, start a yawn fest.

Come on now, tell me – not because you were bored, I hope – but you yawned at least once while reading this, didn't you?

The power of suggestion wins another one.

15

52 Pick Up
For Thella

It took years of listening to those close to me to learn the type of lettuce I bought was not the best. "No flavor," "Rots too fast," and just plain "Yuck" are a few of the remarks that were lovingly conveyed to me. It was suggested I buy just one of those packs of romaine lettuce hearts to see the difference. Oh, I was assured that once I tried romaine, I would leave iceberg in the dust. Or in the mush. HAHA

It all tastes like, well, it all tastes like lettuce to me. I apparently don't have a discerning enough palette to differentiate the delicate differences of the varieties of lettuces. But – yes, a leafy but – to keep peace on the Hidden Valley Ranch, I now buy the packages of romaine lettuce hearts. Big deal, huh? Not really, but here, as per usual, is the rest of this soggy lettuce saga.

After driving 242 miles to Reno for appointments, my husband and I stopped by the grocery store to pick up a load of groceries on the way back home. Shop, shop, shopping we went. I start in the back of grocery stores. I have learned that even though the produce is usually up front, I don't have to get my produce first. If I start in the front, when I get done shopping, I find the tomatoes have gotten run over by the canned corn, or kicked around by a grumpy box of rice.

Just as a side – How lucky are we that we live in a time and in a country where we can buy a watermelon in December? Or corn on the cob in February? Lucky Louies is what we are. Munching on November's celery, let's move along.

After picking over the melons and aforementioned tomatoes, the last thing on my list was the package of romaine lettuce hearts. To my surprise, this super store that touts having everything anyone could ever need was out of lettuce. *All* lettuce. Not a fresh leaf to be had. Well, my other half chased down a produce guy – I mean, seriously chased him down clear into the back room. Why is it that the back room of a grocery store seems to be such a place of mystery? Moving on.

"No fresh lettuce today," the guy reported, motioning to a few, much-handled packages of organic, rust-spotted lettuce. I passed on the overpriced "organic" has-beens, deciding instead on stopping at a second store on the way out of town to pick up a few packages of the obnoxious lettuce.

At the second store, my other half decided he'd had enough shopping, so I zipped in alone to grab the lettuce – and that's when it happened.

While standing at the array of lettuce, I realize that this store got their lettuce shipment that day because they have a mountain of the leafy stuff – head, butter, green leaf, red leaf, arugula, and the ever-elusive packages of three stalks of hearts of romaine. Since I was only going to get the lettuce, I didn't opt for a cart as I came in the door. Poor choice as it turns out. I grabbed three packages and headed for the cashier, remembering that this store was a club and that I needed my club card to check out.

I have, in the past, been caught at the checkout counter trying feverishly to find this store's card. I don't frequently shop at this particular grocery store, so the card is not used enough to garner a top slot in my wallet. Holding three slick packages of lettuce, I started the treasure hunt. Then it happened. All the buyers' club cards I have accumulated over the years slipped out of their designated holder, skittering across the floor of the produce department. And there I was. My life in club cards lay there in a line from the avocados to the zucchini. Ah geez. Of course, I looked around to see if anyone had seen my bumble. There were other shoppers, but they had obviously once been in this position themselves because, with heads bowed, they scurried in all directions like spilled beans on a tile floor.

I began picking up those pieces of plastic as if I was playing the legendary game 52-Card Pickup. It was then that I decided I had become a club-card hoarder. Grocery stores, clothing stores, box stores, hotels, airlines, car rental facilities, home improvement stores, restaurants. Instore, online, and by mail, they all seemed to scream "Use me!"

Oh, I bought the lettuce with the card – saved ten cents – and shuffled from the store, my dignity still wallowing in the middle of the produce section.

I have to admit though it isn't all bad to join a club. I once bought enough Diet Coke over a six-month period to earn a free cruise. Choose your clubs wisely.

16

Fire Building 101
For Emma

I talked to a friend the other day who is about to celebrate 48 years of marriage. Naturally, she was excited so we both gabbed about our numerous years of wedded bliss – my other half and I were due to celebrate 40-plus years ourselves. Marriage is the one job in life that you go into where no experience is required. For instance…

It's getting to be that time of the year. The nights are growing cooler and the mornings brisker. So that means that it's fire-building season. Uh, let me clarify: build a wood fire – in our wood stove – in the mornings – in our house. Like many in our neck of the woods, we supplement our heating with a wood stove. There truly is nothing like a wood fire to warm your backside. Just sit and remember the last camp fire you were around. That instant feeling of heat coming through your shirt to sting your back and then turning around and the heat fluffs its way up to your face and you can feel your cheeks sucking up the BTUs getting you all, well, red in the face. Ah, fall, it has so many facets to it.

Every year it takes about a month to get back into the groove of being able to build the perfect fire in the mornings. Setting the kindling – we use old newspapers. Arranging the wood – we use one piece of wood from a real tree and one sawdust-pressed and paper-covered store-bought log. We used to use only real tree wood, but have found that with age comes the need for ease. Then, my favorite part – lighting the fire and hearing that *woof, woof, woof* of heat being created. If we use these little zoomer logs, as I call them, our real wood will last a lot longer.

Setting a fire correctly is a learned art. Or so I have been told time and time again. We differ, my other half and I, on just how to get the stove going in the morning. We look at it all together differently. He advises one piece of paper, a stick of wood laid in the stove from side to side, and then one of our pressed log-thingies laying from front to back across the wood. This way – again, so I have been told – air will get under the logs so the fire starts better and keeps going.

My way? Munched up paper first, wood from front to back with the pressed log-thingy side to side so it lights easily. I have come to believe that it's because I'm left-handed and he's right-handed that *he* does things so backwards. There is no earthly reason to put the log-thingy clear to the back of the stove where it's harder to light, unless you are right-handed. Maybe it is easier to reach into our stove and light the fire toward the back with your right hand than it is with your left. I wouldn't know as I, again, am left-handed.

So, the first person up in the morning is designated the fire starter. Depending on just how cold it is, I am first up. I get to do my little fire dance as I set the fire and light the zoomer log lying side to side. But then comes the fiddling with the damper. There are two. Well, of course there are.

One damper is on the front of the stove and swivels open and closed while the other is in the stove pipe and turns with a squeak and a crunch of something inside the pipe. Now – again, as I have been told – to get the fire going just right, you need to understand thermal dynamics. This includes how air fuels fire, at what rate the air and fuel mixes, and the angle the air hits the wood and goes over and under the pieces causing an updraft... Why did I have to marry a pilot?

I am what pilots would call a seat-of-the-pants kind of gal. Pull back on the stick and *go!*

With that same frame of mind, I just light the paper in the stove and let the fire go. *Wheeeee.* Fires and airplanes, now there are two things that really have no business being explained in the same breath.

So, we differ on the fire building. That is the married way. The trick isn't in getting the fire going; really, anyone can get a fire going. No, the real trick is in keeping it going, year after fire-building-season year. Never stop stoking the flames.

Wink. Wink.

17

Breakers and Fixers
For Roland

In life there are those of us who constantly break things.
Cars, chairs, doors, sewing machines, tractors, water hydrants… And
then there are those who fix things. Like cars, chairs, doors, sewing
machines, tractors, water hydrants, and deep-fat fryers.

We received a large deep-fat fryer as a wedding gift from a
very nice couple. It was huge. This big ole monster took about half a
gallon of oil to fill it up, so I didn't use it often.

This was way before those turkey deep fryers that are so
common now. And because of my experience with this fryer, I never
wanted to stuff a turkey into hot oil. I just want to shove it in the
oven and let that heavenly turkey aroma fill the house and then put
my back out trying to lift the heavy sucker out of the oven when it is
done. I'm just saying.

But on occasion, when we hungered for French fries and the
closest place to buy them was over 70 miles away, I filled the lovely,
avocado-green thing up and fried away. About the third time I dug it
out from under the counter, filled it up with oil, and plugged it in, it
refused to heat up.

I fiddled with the plug, as we women do. I unplugged it and
plugged it back in. I wiggled the cord where it went into the
appliance. But still no heat. I thought I would have to throw it out as
that was how broken things were handled in my before-I-was-
married home with my parents.

Then, my new husband came home and saw my plight.
Without hesitation, he said he would take a look at it. Well, I had
already done the plug thing. I had even bounced the fryer, ever so

gently, on the counter. What else did he think he could do? I washed it out and got it un-oiled so he could "take a look." I was amazed at what happened next.

He turned it upside down, and began to unscrew the bottom.

What? Nobody is supposed to *ever* unscrew the bottom. Why, that would be like putting a knife into a toaster. "You could *die*," I remarked while standing a safe distance away.

Hadn't he read the "WARNING! WARNING!" emblazoned and engraved on the black plastic bottom of the fryer and also on the colorful tag attached to the cord!

He just laughed, his hands never slowing. Once the bottom was off, we peered into the space of wires and coils. *Wow.* I had never seen the innards of an appliance. Or, I might add, the innards of a cow or a sheep or a chicken... Those innards would also become part of my as-seen-on-the-farm repertoire sooner or later.

"Well, here's the problem. This wire has come undone from the heating coil," my other half announced. He grabbed a little yellow, plastic thingy, which I have come to know as a wire nut, screwed the two unhooked wires together, replaced the bottom of the fryer, and handed it back to me. I knew at that moment that I had married the right guy.

From that day forward when something breaks, and there have been many, many broken-all-by-themselves items along the way. HAHA I just have to say "Fix it" and – *presto!* – it's fixed. Yes, I have, on occasion, had to bat my baby blues his way. I am one luck, luck, lucky lady. Now, I tell you that story to make this next part more poignant.

One day after many years of watching Mr. Fix-it, I took it upon myself to think I could fix an antique brass-bladed fan I had found in one of our many storage sheds. It was hot and we did not have a swamp cooler or air conditioning. Did I say it was hot? Well, it was. Maybe not fry-an-egg-on-the-sidewalk hot, but it was definitely melt-a-cherry-popsicle-faster-than-you-can-slurp-it-down-to-the-stick hot.

Farming was in full swing. Mr. Fix-It was really busy and I felt like after years of watching things be repaired, I could fix this fan. After all, it had a cord and a motor; it spun when I stuck my finger in the cage where the blades were. Really, how hard could this be?

Oh, and it was hot that day. Did I mention that?

So, after finding that the fan did not work when plugged in, and doing my oh-so-scientific plug wiggling, I grabbed a screwdriver, hammer, pliers, black electrical tape, a glass of iced tea, and dug right in.

Do you have any idea how many parts are on an antique brass-bladed fan that also has the ability to oscillate when operational?

Well, my friends, there are more than ten, but not many less than a thousand parts and pieces. From my standpoint, it was just a little 12-inch fan – *why were there sooooo many parts?* Had to be that some of them were non-essential, right?

By the time Mr. Fix-It walked in the door, I had every single screw unscrewed, each part un-parted from the fan, and strewn across every part of the eight-foot kitchen counter.

Why he ever stayed and put up with me I have no idea to this day…

He calmly picked up the tools, put the poor little thing back together, plugged it in, cooled us both off… and then hid all tools from me. Putting them *all* under lock and key. Yeah, I thought that last part was a bit overkill.

Now you know – in life, there are breakers and there are fixers. I am a breaker. If you too are a breaker, do not kid yourself into thinking that you are a fixer. Just go with the knowledge you are what you are and reveille in it. If not, you could find yourself one fine day alone, without thinking, dangerously walking toward that toaster – with a knife.

18

Don't Touch

For Margaret

There is a commercial on television of late that shows, presumably, a zoo keeper throwing meat to lions. Big lions. The kind of lions that make me think, "If they didn't have claws, I would really like to touch them." But alas, they do have claws, and teeth, and enough strength to rip limbs off dang-near anything. But still, I would like to pet them, run my hand along their warm fur. I wouldn't want to wear their fur as a coat, mind you. That just doesn't appeal to me. But like little cats, these big cats got me thinking...

Why are there things in our existence that are seeable but untouchable?

My favorite animal is the hippo. I just think little hippos are adorable. They, of course, do grow up to become *big* hippos that swim under water in rivers where I think they grab their prey by the legs and drag them under and eat them. Hippos are the most notorious of jungle animals. But baby hippos are cuties. I have to move on to where I am going with all this.

We just acquired a pack of kittens – nine in all, a nice round number. I really like kittens and cats. Guess that is why the commercial with the big lions grabbed me. These kittens were a bit on the skittish side, but I knew after a few days of warm, Trina affection, and, uh, gobs of food and treats, they would come around. I'm good at taming, but I know food does more good than my oh-so-warm-and-lovely "Here kitty, kitty."

True to form, the little balls of fur started to calm down – all except for this one fuzzy little guy. Of course, he was the one I really want to pick up. Why was that? Nine to choose from and the one I had set my eyes on runs at the mere sight of my big ole clod-hopper feet coming toward him. I just want to hold him and give him squishes – *it's not what it sounds like!* I don't squish until their eyes nearly pop out. Thankfully, I outgrew that when I was two. I just wanted him to know he was safe and loved. But that little bugger ran away with his tail just a'flicking at me as if to say, "*Hee, hee, hee!* I have this beautiful black, fuzzy hair and I can outrun you, old lady."

I resorted to the underhanded tactics I have acquired over my many years of kitten-taming. Usually, I wait until the babies are all lined up slurping at their warm milk mush and then I pet them. I can have my pick of the litter – pun intended. But this Fuzzy Wuzzy was having none of that. He waited me out. I felt sorry for him not getting any warm goodness, so I just walked away. I tried the left-hand wiggling while the right hand grabbed, but the little guy must have eyes in the back of his fuzzy little head because he scampered away just before I was ready to nab him.

He appeared to be winning. Until yesterday. I finally beat the little critter at his own game. I was aloof, unresponsive to his taunting little kitten meow. I let him think I was in no way interested in grabbing him and squishing him any longer. I sat on the back deck on my favorite tree stump log that I had brought home from the forest from a vacation long ago and let all the kittens do kitten stuff while I just sat. Watching and waiting. Then he came closer, closer. I had had just enough caffeine to give me the edge...

Like a big cat myself, I flew into pounce mode. I had him! I was the victor – Nope, he was. He had 20 claws and many, many teeth and let out a growl that came from the tip of his tail. Holy cats and kittens, Batman, was he ever a handful! But years of kitten-taming has taught me that if you hold kittens by the nap of the neck like their mothers do, you can put them in what I call "neutral" and get the upper hand. So, neutral it was. Worked like a charm. Now, Fuzzy is my friend, until tomorrow when we start all over again with "Don't touch me!"

Just a note…

I need to tell you here that sometimes I am wrong. When I am wrong, I get a note from a reader telling me I am wrong. I do not take offense to that. I know – trust me here – I know I am not the smartest person in the room. I have never thought I was and I would never want to be. Too much pressure. I am more of a fly-by-the-seat-of-my-pants gal.

So, what was I wrong about? Well, it seems that hippos, still my favorite jungle animal, only eat plants – not people. They don't swim underwater, grab you by the legs, and eat you. But they usually do not appreciate you swimming in their pool. If you tick them off – which apparently happens often in Africa – they will swim underwater, grab you by the legs, and maybe, possibly, all things considered, they will kill you…

But they will not eat you.

Good to know, huh?

19

Highway Bicycling
For Mike Z.

Apparently bicycling across Nevada on US Highway 50, which was dubbed "The Loneliest Road" in America some 30-plus years ago (July 1986) in *Life Magazine*, gives the bicyclist a grand notch on their bicycling pants belt. Right next to the notch that marks the accomplishment of completing a trip of biking some over-the-rainbow road. Or getting a bronze badge in the shape of a 1950 Schwinn for crossing the great divide on a bike.

I am not without awe at these road warriors. How do you get the gumption to look at a map, decide that sometime during the hottest time of the year you will climb aboard a bicycle with a tiny, tiny seat and very skinny tires – a bike that, in most cases, is usually only used to get you from your house to your friend's house because you are too young to drive – and then ride some 250-plus miles over tall and steep mountain passes and across long and wide valleys. Remarkable, to say the least!

It is so foreign to me. It's like if someone was to tell me that I would really enjoy beating myself about the head and shoulders with a large stick and I run crazily to the nearest fallen log, pull off a wayward stick, and begin beating myself about said head and shoulders. No, I'm pretty sure I wouldn't do that – or bike The Loneliest Road. But – yes, there's a "but" coming…and it is on a tiny, tiny seat – but I am in awe of those hardy, ambitious souls.

Okay, picture this. We were driving west from Eureka, Nevada to Reno on a wonderful early September day and ran across a group of bicyclists, a string of peddlers that strung out for over 100 miles doing The Loneliest Road gallivant. One or two at a time, they peddled up a rise with determination or coasted down a grade with a hardy smile on their weary faces. Taking the 240-plus mile adventure with those bicyclists were the supporting staff and their vehicles.

Now, this is where it gets interesting – honest.

When you pass a support car (which you can identify by its slow speeds, hand-painted "slow-moving vehicle" signs, and all matter of bicycling gear dripping off the top and back) it is comforting to know that the cyclists are being cared for. If the support cars are stopped, you can read the multitude of signs that adorn their cars and spot resting cyclists getting shade, nutrition, water, and a hardy "Atta boy." It really is quite an amazing and well-orchestrated attraction. *But…*

The major summit on Nevada's Highway 50 Loneliest Road is Austin Summit. A long and steep climb no matter how you look at it. Going east or west, Austin Summit is the halfway point between Fallon, Nevada and Ely, Nevada – the starting and/or stopping points of this wonder-filled 268-mile ride. As you climb the mountain to Austin Summit, you can see the crest looming up ahead.

As we ascended to the top, we noticed a support vehicle perpendicular to the road with its tailgate open. Close to the edge of the road was a brightly colored canvas shade erected along its west side to guard against the brutal sun. As we approached, we spotted a pile of brownish something or other lying, unmoving in the sun, alongside this vehicle. While we couldn't see any stopped bicyclist, or support staff waiting in anticipation, we could see this lumpy mass. Being well-traveled Nevadans, we thought someone had maybe hit a deer and the poor thing was still there in a heap. As we drew closer, the brown lump took a more interesting shape. A *girlish* shape. A very, uh, tanned-and-nearly-unclothed shape. What we had happened upon was a buxom, bikini-clad young gal lying on a blanket sunning herself along The Loneliest Road in America.

Now, a zillion things could have happened at that juncture. Several quips could have been quipped. Facts and fiction could have abound from this passing. It was just the two of us in our car – a man and a woman, a yin-yang, so to speak. A Mars and a Venus.

Or… In other words… one of us saw the bikini while the other just saw a brown lump. Made for an interesting next 110 miles to the next pit stop.

I wonder what Nevada nuggets were uttered in other passing cars or by bikers while surviving the Loneliest Road in America.

20

Not to But In, But...

For Eleny

I'm going to get right to it.

Nothing good can come of a conversation when your first sentence begins with, "Okay, don't get mad – but…"

Right off the bat, the little hairs on the back of your neck show some sign of life by standing straight up. When someone says to you, "Don't get mad, but…" there is a 99 percent chance that what they are about to say will make you mad as a wet hen without a comb.

If you hear, "Okay, don't get upset – but…" you might as well get it into your head that you're going to get upset. Probably upset enough to lose some sleep no matter how many sheep are waiting on your pillow to be counted.

Of course, there are several of these sentence beginnings that should be avoided.

"Okay, don't get all excited, *but*…"

"Okay, don't let this ruin your day, *but*…"

"Okay, don't let me rain on your parade, *but*…"

I have been on both ends of these sentence startings. Experience has taught me that whether you are delivering or receiving them, there is zero chance of a good outcome. But me being me, I have admittedly delivered more than I have received. For instance…

Okay hon, don't get mad, *but*… I just found your wallet – in the washing machine – again.

Okay, don't get upset, but that extra money we were saving for vacation will have to go toward fixing the garage door that, for some reason, didn't go all the way up before I backed the truck out of the garage.

And by the way, do you know how much a new camper shell back window costs? With new hinges and those cute hold-up-the-window thingies?

Okay, husband of mine, don't get all excited, but the tractor wheel has this liquid stuff coming out of it and it looks a little flat…

In my defense, that last one wasn't my fault. The tractor wheel rusted through, causing the liquid stuff, which is put into tractor tires to add weight and traction, to leak out. It just so happened that it started to leak at the time I was using the tractor to move some dirt to fill in yet another hole the dog had dug in the garden.

So, not my fault.

Neither was the hole the dog dug – unless you count the fact that I left the garden gate open, again.

Honestly, it's the word "but" that seems to be the problem. "But" has a sneaky way of splitting a pretty good sentence into one that, well, isn't so wonderful. Like, "I love you, but…"

Or, "No, that dress doesn't make you look like you just fell off the turnip truck, but…"

See?

If the word "but" was banned, these types of sentences would have no chance of finishing. But stopping before a "but" comes out of your mouth – *now, there's a unique visual* – is harder than trying to gather up a dropped egg from the kitchen floor before the dog gets to it to slurp it up.

Of course, as in every tale, there are two sides. Therefore, there are two sides of a "but." Another questionable visual. Like saying, "I love you, but there is no way that such a great person as you could ever love me." Ah, see how sweet your "but" can turn out to be?

Even the washing machine "but" can be given a new slant. For instance, you might say, "Now, don't get mad. I found your wallet in the washing machine again, but now you don't have to worry about hiding that old picture of your last girlfriend behind the picture of your mother anymore!"

That is one "but" several females might possibly find a use for! You're welcome!

All in all, I think the concept of "buts" could use some work. Just consider taking a few minutes each day to work on the placement of your "buts."

You might even find that it is in your best interest to only use your "but" for good.

But then again…

21

The Wind-Up
For J.P.

More times than I can count I want to start a column with "Picture this!" But that line is overused and I simply don't want to be cliché. So, try as I might to come up with some other remarkably catchy lines, today I just have to say, "Picture this!"

I was recently at a jewelry counter, although I was not there to buy jewelry – even though there might have been just the tiniest drop of drool on the left side of my mouth as I looked through the showcase glass at a pair of platinum and diamond earrings that would have lit my face up like nobody's business! But no, I wasn't there to buy jewelry. I was there to buy a watch battery for my other half's fancy timepiece which used a unique battery.

I asked for the battery by number – a 687-BFD, I think, but don't hold me to it. The gal knew exactly what I needed and turned to draw one from the safe. Apparently, it was a *very* exclusive battery. She returned to me and asked to see my watch with the obvious intention of installing the battery for me.

Since the battery was not for my watch but for my other half's, I thought it might be kinda fun to play with the clerk, so I slid my watch off my wrist. It has one of those metal, stretchy won't-catch-your-arm-hair-and-pull-them-out-by-the-roots band. Seemingly disgusted, the clerk gave me a look to suggest I was committing some sort of jewelry faux-pas. In my world, a foo-*pah*!

So, the gal got out her little six-by-twelve-inch padded piece of counter rug and smoothed it with her hand like it was made of mink and not fake velvet. She took my watch with a delicate, but heavily-bejeweled, borrowed-from-the-store diamond-ring-wearing hand and reached for her jewel-encrusted eye loop. I think I snickered a little at her show and what I knew was to come.

Next, she reached under the counter and pulled out a dark purple bundle tied with well-used, lavender ribbon which she ceremoniously untied. She unrolled the cloth to reveal an impressive line of watchmaker's tools. With her tools laid out before her, she whined, "Well, let's just see what we can do for this watch, shall we?"

Again, admittedly, I snickered. Her little boney fingers picked up the watch and turned it over to reveal a scratched back panel. She then brought the eye loop next to her eye, squinting to hold it in place. At this point I should've said the battery was not for my watch. I should've said it was for my husband's watch. I should've… but I didn't. She needed to learn a lesson; she needed to learn to talk to the customer, ask questions, and be aware, not condescending.

She examined the watch, turning it back and forth, up and down. "I don't see how to get the back off. Is this an older model?"

I couldn't go on any more. Trying to keep a solemn expression, I said, "The battery isn't for this watch, it's for my husband's. This watch doesn't use a battery."

Then things took a turn that even I couldn't have seen coming… Miss twenty-something looked up at me and remarked, "Wow, no battery! How does it keep running?" Really? I took it from her and started to *wind it up*! I honestly don't think she had ever seen a watch that you wind-up. She didn't even know what I was doing until I showed her my old, wind-up-every-morning Timex from the Stone Age!

The battery was $47.95; I'm still not sure why it was deemed "safe" material. I can say that that silly battery cost more than twice the amount I had paid for my watch in the olden days. But the look on her face? *Priceless*. See you next "time!" Sorry just couldn't help myself…

22

Have You Seen My Sunglasses?
For Candy

The sun drives me crazy. My skin comes from a long line of glow-in-the-dark, light-skinned, nearly transparent Europeans. The kind of people that might have been used to light up the stage for Vaudeville plays. Yes, that bright.

So, when summer begins its imminent approach, I need to start wearing my shorts as early as I can without freezing my knees off. This is so I can gain a bit of color before going out into heavily traveled public spaces.

This year was no different. But this year, I decided to do something about my "farmer's tan." You know, the tan you get when you constantly wear short sleeves so your arms from about three inches above your elbows down to your hands get sun and turn a nice crispy brown but from the bottom of your sleeve up, there is skin that only sees light when you take a shower! I proudly say I have a *great* farmer's tan. This year though, I was going to try to toughen up and brown up my glow-in-the-dark shoulders. But first, I needed to find my sunglasses so I could go outside with my eyes open.

See, there's something in me that tends to space out occasionally. So far, I've not become a space cadet during anything really important like driving or ironing something delicate. No, I tend to space out about *where* I put things.

Just the other day, I went to the post office where I use a key to get into my mail box… Then my keys disappeared. Just *vanished*. I remember having them. I must have because I got my mail all the way home. But the keys decided to take a mini vacation. I went back the next day to ask about the keys, but no keys had been turned in. For security reasons, I don't put my name on them.

Pretty smart, I told myself – I put my P.O. Box number on them. Quite clever, huh?

Wait…

…

…

After seeing that written out, maybe that's not such a good idea.

So, with that anecdote revealed, I feel emboldened to say – my sunglasses have disappeared. Oh, I've looked for them. In the house, car, truck, shop, garage, on the lawn mower.

I've checked to see if they were stuck in the hammock, checked to see if they had fallen off my head into the cat box during cleaning. Not there, thank goodness!

It wouldn't be so bad if they were normal sunglasses, but alas, they were prescription.

To my chagrin, I was forced to drive to Twin Falls, Idaho without them. At the first pharmacy I came to, I bought these little spring-designed, hook-over-my-regular-glasses shades. They lasted about a day. The spring sprung – or would that be sprang? – and the spring was pushed too far during a fight I had with them. I don't think I was supposed to twang them as far as they would go. Oh well, there's $14.99 plus tax down the pooper shoot.

So, I remained on the hunt for my faithful sunglasses. They *had* to be somewhere. I knew they fell off because I had perched them atop my head for so long that they too are sprung out of kilter (again, would that be sprang?) to stay on top of my nicely rounded head.

I know, I know. "Don't put your glasses on your head" is the mantra of my doctor's eyeglasses sales woman. But did I listen? Nope! I just kept going in to have them tightened. Last time I got *the* look, the look that said they will no longer work on them. They said I needed new ones.

Imagine that. I think mine are only about nine years old. Yeah, I guess I got my money's worth!

Exactly where, when you lose your glasses, do you look? Because I've exhausted all the avenues. They weren't in the bathroom. Kitchen. Bedroom. Under the couch cushions. It will be more than interesting to discover where they are – *if* I ever find them.

I'm batting 500 though. I went to the post office today and in my box, which I had to open with my just-in-case key that I hang on the rear-view mirror, were my post office keys. *Hurray.*

Some kind soul had found them carousing out and about and had turned them in, and – I'd like to add because I had the forethought to put my box number on them – the gals at the post office were able to place them back in the box for me.

I want to thank the wonderful person who found them and ask kindly, if they could, to find my dang sunglasses!

23

The Standard Transmission
For Tracie

Drivers Education. Words that make the heart of a 15-year-old jump with joy while shivering in fear. That is when Drivers Ed was offered to wannabe drivers in my high school. Now, I must admit, since Drivers Ed is no longer a course in many schools, I do not know how youngsters learn to drive these days. Parents are, of course, the first line of teaching. I can just see parents, huddled around a kitchen table in the middle of the night. It is dark and quiet and a little chilly. Mom has hold of the kitchen-corn broom, stems up and handle down. Dad has pulled out two pieces of the straw and holds them, exposed ends equal in height, tight fisted in his hand.

"Agreed," Dad says, "short stick loses." She pulls one out and hides her choice until he reveals his. They compare and he yips; mom whimpers. She has pulled the short straw. She will be the driving teacher of their teenaged child who will be getting a driver's permit and will need to be taught the ins and outs of driving. That is, just as soon as the written test is passed.

The written test? Yes, the written test.

I accidentally let my license expire a few years ago which, when that happens, means you have to take the written test. *Swell.* That day I had the grand opportunity to take up number 85 at the DMV just as number 42 was announced. I sat and began my wait, taking in all the goings on around me. I must admit that the most fun was watching the kids take their written tests in a roped off area of the room. A few of us were patient while others without thought of these test takers felt it important to complain loudly… very loudly.

What exactly does complaining and uttering disgruntled remarks get you? Does the line move faster?

Don't get me started.

Let's just keep driving ahead keeping our hands on the wheel at ten and two. HAHA

The written test is mostly common-sense stuff, but it is a rite of passage. I still remember taking it the first time some 40-plus years ago. More importantly, I remember the two questions I missed. The first was about which way to turn the wheels when parking on a hill; the other was about what a yellow triangle-shaped sign stands for.

Fifty-fifty was the chance on the wheels – I guessed wrong.

The sign, which I said meant yield, in reality, was caution. To this day, I say yield means caution. But the instructor, Mr. Pearce, wouldn't budge.

I got my learner's permit anyway and, to my mother's chagrin, was on my way to becoming a driver.

"Hide the women and children," was what my dad said!

The dirt road going out to Lackawanna, an old spring north of town, was my proving ground. Now, it is a major paved road that leads to the maximum-security Nevada State Prison near Ely, Nevada. Is there a connection there? Naw.

To Mom's credit, or maybe it was the Prozac, she was calm, cool, and collected. I learned to drive in the family's T-bird. Automatic transmission. Electric everything, even wing windows. I had taken Drivers Ed so I knew the basics, but needed a bit of real road work. The six months between 15½ and 16, when in Nevada you can get a duly-certified driver's license, went pretty quickly. Soon, heart pounding in my throat, I was taking the driving part of the test with that same DMV agent in the passenger seat. Off in the T-bird we went.

Upon returning to the little white building that housed the DMV, I parked and turned the wheels, the wrong way again. We exited the car and with a stern face, Mr. Pearce said I had passed. My picture taken and the laminating done, I was issued my license.

The jest of this story? That night with new license in hand, I set off to drive my friends up and down main street and cause havoc and commotion within the community but – and that is a *big* but – we didn't go cruising in that T-Bird! Nope, I got the family's old 1966 Plymouth Barracuda, a fine red car – with a standard transmission. Three speed on the column; no problem. *Yeah right.* I knew in my mind how it worked. But getting it to work was the problem. So, there I was in a car full of giggling 15 and 16-year-old girls driving most of the evening in first gear, slowing as much as possible at each red light praying it would turn green before we got there so that the darn clutch wouldn't be needed.

We ground on that tranny so much, I am sure if it was a meat grinder, we would have ground a ton of hamburger by the end of the night.

I'm also pretty sure on a quiet summer night in that small Eastern Nevada town, they can still hear that poor six-cylinder engine revving in first gear and the *chunk-a-chug*, *chunk-a-chug* of the standard transmission being pushed to its limits.

Thanks to my brother, I now know what the friction point on a standard tranny is.

Thanks, Rod!

24

No Tell Hotel
For Debbie

I am not an ostrich. I do not live with my head in the sand. I watch enough television to know that things go on in hotel rooms that I don't want to know about. Most importantly, I am not naive enough to think that I am the first person to stay in the room I have just rented. With that said, here is what happened during a recent hotel stay.

So *tra la la, tra la la*, we left our room on our way to dinner. This was a nice hotel, kind of what you would think was up-scale.

FYI – we have spent several nights of our lives in, shall we say, more than a few pegs down from the top ten lists of motels. Yes, the kind where you don't even want to take your shoes off. I digress…

As we walked down the hall toward the elevators of our hotel, another guest approached us and asked nonchalantly if we were staying in room number XXX. He passed us to slide his key card into the door a few down from our room. "Yes," we said, not thinking anything of it. He goes on to tell us that he had stayed in our room for the previous two weeks and that it was a great room.

What?

We politely acknowledged that it was indeed a nice room and left. In the elevator, my other half and I exchanged looks of *ew*.

This quite unassuming encounter opened in me a whole new line of thoughts. On our way out to dinner, we discussed the encounter. We speculated about who he was, why he had stayed in a hotel for weeks, and how he could afford to stay for an extended period of time in *this* hotel. The nightly rate we were paying had forced us to opt for a meal delivered to us through a drive-up window rather than a nice, sit-down dinner with cloth napkins and a hostess.

When we returned to the hotel, we were less anxious to enter our room than when we had originally been once checked in. I, of course, checked the closets to make sure we were still the only two in there. I still couldn't convince myself that there wasn't some way he could use his key card from the week before. Unrealistic as that sounds.

Just let it go, Trina, I told myself. I know I was not the first person to stay in this really nice room. But still… I don't want to know who was there before me. I don't want to know anything about them.

Upon visiting our bathroom, I happened to look at the whirlpool tub/shower. I was no longer interested in it. Prior to our *encounter*, I had thought about filling the tub and getting jetted into relaxation. But the guy who had had the room before me had tainted it. A quick shower was all I could muster.

After a bit of television, it was time for bed. Now here, I let my CSI television watching almost get the best of me. Almost. At every hotel, our routine before bed includes taking off the bedspread or duvet or whatever they have covering the bed. We have, for some time, brought our own blankets; his is brown and mine is blue and we…

Well, this is one of those things you just don't need or probably want to know about the previous guests who stayed in your room before you.

So, I put my head on the pillow and tried not to think about which side of the bed our previous guest had slept on. Suddenly, my husband said, "Did you ever think about the pillows and how many people have breathed into them over the life of the pillow?" In the end, even though the pillow case was clean and crisp and smelled okay, I couldn't use it. It found a home across the room on the floor.

So *please*, my friends, take to heart my plight lest it happen to you.

Do not tell me or anyone where you have slept – even though it might be somewhat cool to read a "Washington Slept Here" plaque displayed in a few B&B's across our country that. I don't want to know that Joe Schmoe from down the hall used my bathroom, made popcorn in my microwave, used my pillow, and lastly, slept in my bed!

Sleep well, I guess.

25

The Blue Box
For Mom

It's Christmas time. A time of good cheer, merriment, and warm fuzzy feelings. I do not forget the reason for the season. The birth of my Savior. But I also am inclined to enjoy the warmth of all that the season offers. Friends, family, food, frivolity, and – decorating! More so in years past, but still I trudge out to the storage shed and retrieve the priceless family decorations. Now, why is this of such importance to write about? What is it that makes this annual event noteworthy? The blue box.

Let me start here. Finding themselves with three small kids, an obligatory sea foam-green family station wagon with faux wood sides, the invent of cherry Kool-Aid, boxes of 64-color crayons, a big dog named Ginger, leaky diapers, and real rubbery rubber pants, my parents had a need for seat covers. In the fifties, Fingerhut, a mail-order company whose specialty was plastic bubble seat covers, was a big thing.

Here is where the blue box started its amazing life.

In 1955 – a very good year – my parents ordered brand new protective seat covers for their car from Fingerhut.

The seat covers were indeed plastic, *clear* plastic, with little raised square globs for decoration and breathability. I feel they were there to discharge static electricity accumulated by your rear end sliding to-and-fro across the seats, assuming it was not summer when any bare skin would adhere to the plastic causing a ripping sound when you tried to exit the car. Apparently, this was what was available before nice soft sheepskin seat covers or seat covers with material that makes your seats look like black and white dairy cows or the ones that let you sit on Betty Boop's face… Wandered off the trail again, didn't I?

But this isn't about the seat covers, as attractive as they were! It is about the box they came in which sported little gold stars on a field of cobalt blue and Fingerhut scrawled across it in big golden letters, a great heavy-duty box about 3 feet long, 18 inches wide and 8 inches deep with a waxy-coated bottom and a lid.

Now, 1955 was a long time ago, so why can I be so precise about this one box out of the many boxes that have crossed my path over the years? Because I still have that box, and still use it. It houses my family Christmas decorations and comes out every year like it has since 1955. It is well-traveled.

I'm going to estimate, not counting the original miles from Minnesota to Nevada, this box has traveled a good mile and a half moving from basements and other storage hidey holes of various family homes to the living room before Christmas and back into storage after the celebration for the past 60-plus years. The box was handed to me by my mother when she moved to Pittsburg, Texas after her and dad both retired and moved out of the snow of Eastern Nevada. A snowless dream I'm sure nearly all of us have.

Now, it's my honor to slip-slide through snow and ice to bring the box of family Christmas' gone by into my house. Which I did this very week. I can still read the label, yellowed and curled on the edges. That is how I know it was from Minnesota. When it originally came, I was not able to read. I was not able to do much more than gurgle, spit up, and use those rubber pants during the Christmas of '55. Now I can run my fingers across the name hand-written by a long-since-gone Fingerhut employee on the label addressed to my dad on Greenbrae Drive, Sparks, Nevada – just a few blocks west of the bowling alley and Uncle Happy's toy store, a store we pined to go to each Friday night, but especially at Christmas time. Now *that* was a toy store. Think Toys-R-Us before steroids.

That blue box holds not only some of my maiden Russell family treasures, but some Machacek family mementoes as well, like his grandparents' hand-blown glass ornaments from the old country and the little plastic Rudolphs that my husband remembers from his childhood. My favorite? My mom's little ceramic bells that came out when *It's A Wonderful Life* was released. In that movie, the big line was "Whenever a bell rings, an angel gets their wings."

So I make sure to ring those little bells every year as I place them on our tree. Maybe that is why it is important to ring in the New Year. *Ting-a-ling.*

26

Feeling Cornered
For Dr. Dan

If idle hands are the devil's workshop, my idle mind finds things to count. I count corners – not to be confused with *cutting* corners, as I do that too. I might not follow a recipe to the nth degree by cutting out or adding some spices, but I *never* cut out the amount of chocolate or butter a recipe calls for. That would be sacrilege. Cutting corners and counting corners are two entirely different things. Cutting is a hands-on thing and counting is a head thing.

Here's how it started. When I was about eight, I was dragged off to visit the dentist. Not like the dentists of today who talk calmly and quietly to the little tykes so as not to cause fear and discontent in them. No, this dentist, as I oh-so-clearly remember him was green, slime-covered, had horns and bugged eyes, and laughed a deep notorious laugh as he lashed me to his yellow, plastic-covered chair. Rubbing his hands together, he drew that pick-thingy with the hook on the end that picks at your teeth into his hand and scratched at my teeth, catching the corner of my teeth as he dragged it along the inside of my mouth. Yeah… *that* dentist!

I'm not blaming anyone but myself for the awful decay inside my mouth. My parents had their hands full with life by the time their third child – me – came along. So, I learned a lot of stuff on my own the hard way. Riding a bike, eating a banana by first peeling it, brushing my teeth. By the time I was of tooth age and school age, I had awful teeth. My first dental visit when I was about eight was when I met Dr. Slimy.

I knew as I walked into his dungeon/office and heard the drilling coming from behind the poorly-painted door covered with little scratch marks from previous children who had tried to escape, along with that shiver-inducing burning tooth smell that I was in trouble. I needed to run! I still get those shivers.

That first visit didn't go well. So much so that I thought I would never have to go back. But go back I did, an event that to this day haunts me and has had a lasting effect on my psyche. I spent four – yes, *four* – hours in what became a very sticky with sweat, yellow chair that day. I still think the amount of money paid for those four hours put Ole Dr. Slimy's perfect-toothed child through at least one semester of college. It put me through a lifetime of, well, here it is – corner counting.

Sitting under the bright light, I tried to close my eyes to the world, but the *zing zing zing* of the drill and the *crick crick crick* of the scrape against my teeth brought me back into the then and there. So, in my struggle to live through the torture, I looked up. Praying? I don't know. Maybe. But I saw that the ceiling of the office had those square panels of ceiling tiles. These were the ones with what looked like dots of holes punched all over them. They were white, well, off-white as they had sucked up years of smoke wafting up from the teeth that dang drill had drilled on! Okay, that's a stretch even for me.

Escaping the goings on in my mouth, I counted those squares. Many times I counted the ones that I could see from my reclined position. That didn't take long. Eight across and six from the wall to as far back as my eyeballs could travel. Over and over I counted.

Then it happened. I started counting the corners of the squares.

1-2-3-4.   1-2-3-4.   1-2-3-4.

Then I got bored so I counted the four corners in each cube that formed an X. As time dragged on, I counted the corners that would be seen on the tops of the tiles, uh, if you were standing in the attic. Oh, this goes on forever.

Finally, I was out of that chair and on my way home, fat lips and all.

The counting did not stop however. I still count – corners of windows, the corners of the TV, corners of corners from the four corners of the world. It's not as nutty as it sounds as I have found out. There are lots of ways to get through situations, but the secret is to be able to turn the corner and just keep going.

27

No-Time Time Zone
For Jamie

There are many time zones around the world. There are four common ones in the continental U.S. On the west coast, we are in the Pacific Time Zone. It works well for us until we need to call the east coast after two in the afternoon. That is when you realize you missed your window of opportunity to talk with that insurance company representative in Hartford, Connecticut or the company that was to ship your new shoes from Georgia. At 2:01 p.m. Pacific Time, they are already on their way home since it is after 5 p.m. on the east coast.

No, if you want to be sure to talk to the east coast, the best thing to do is to get up and be on the phone at 6 a.m. Pacific Time which would be just at 9 a.m. or right after coffee and just before lunch for the easterners. You think we have it bad? Just think how early the people in Hawaii have to get up to call the east coast on business.

Do we really feel bad for those poor people living in the paradise we call Hawaii? Sun, surf, little paper umbrellas everywhere! They can fend for themselves!

With that being said, I have come across a startling realization – we are all living in the *same* time zone. Not the pacific, mountain, central, eastern, or even Hawaiian time zones. (For those who don't know it, Hawaii is in the Aleutian time zone (AST) which is two hours earlier than the Pacific.)

No, with all the things needing to get done in our ever-shortening days, I've decided that we all live in the No-Time Time Zone.

For example, even though the advertisement used to say there is always time for Jell-O, we now seem to have become so busy we need to buy our Jell-O already made, packaged, and ready to gobble down while we zip to our next appointment. What happened to mixing the powder with water and stuffing it into our refrigerators? I know, it all started when Jell-O came out with the speed method of preparation. Instead of adding boiling water then cold water, the speed method encouraged us to mix ice in with the cold water allowing the Jell-O to set faster. Why do we need our Jell-O to set up faster? What happened to the time when we had to wait for our Jell-O to jell?

I admire mothers with babies, school-age children, *and* a job. Wow, they truly are magicians. They find time hiding in the most remarkable ways. I spied one such mom holding a baby, handing out crackers to another toddler, and filling out papers for a doctor's appointment, all while talking on the phone and looking through her purse for a tissue to wipe the corners of her mouth as she had just swallowed the last bite of her yummy drive-thru lunch. She was the epitome of the No-Time Time Zone inhabitant.

Men too have been there. My other half just wrote a list of his tomorrow schedule. Business needs, neighbor needs, yard work, automobile needs, household needs, doctors' appointments. So, you see, this No-Time Time Zone is universal.

The only humans that do not notice that there is not enough time are small children, the ones that are still grabbing the crackers handed out by strung-out mothers. Lucky little tikes. High school-aged kids are vaguely aware that something is changing. They are close enough to feel the pull of the No-Time Time Zone, slowly becoming aware of that timely gnaw to be at the next class, game, date, party, or work if they have it. However, they still have a full tank of energy to dip into. We more mature adults often look at our fuel gauges and see the red needle bouncing on "E."

There are times – I know you will find this hard to believe – when I have been asked if I have an off button. Quit your snickering!

Apparently, I do *not* have an off button or I would not be touting the fact that we live in the No-Time Time Zone.

How do we find our off buttons? More importantly, how do we push them once we find them? Maybe a nap is our off button. The only thing I have found wrong with the whole nap process as an adult is that we don't get cookies and milk first. Luckily, lying on the floor on a little rug has been upgraded to stretching out on a soft, comfy couch!

Now, go eat your pre-packaged green Jell-O and get busy.

28

Carrying the Torch
For Matthew

It's cosmic that the more you are told you can't have, can't do, aren't allowed to, or are not invited to, the more you want to go, do, be, and have. I know because I have, for some time now, wanted to learn how to run a cutting torch. Yes, a cutting torch. The one piece of equipment in our machine shop that I have yet to feel the power of use. For those who do not know what it is, let me tell you that it involves fire, *hot fire*. Sparks, lots of sparks. Heating iron and bending it with your bare hands can make you feel like Superman – well, by grabbing the red-hot iron with a pair of pliers since it will be hot enough to not only fry an egg, but flesh. Ye-ouch!

Oh, I have welded. I have cut with a power saw. Run a lathe. Sand-blasted years of stuff off of things that are greasy, painted, and just plain icky. I know where all the hand, air, and power tools are and about what 99 percent of them do. I can hand pack a wheel bearing and change oil in a truck. And, of course, I have had the honor of being the one to run a broom. I am really good at running a broom. I said *run* a broom not *ride* a broom. HAHA But that shiny brass torch with all its levers and knobs? It is elusive still, after some 40 years.

I feel I am a reasonably safe person. I look both ways before crossing my fingers. I count to ten before I lift with my knees. I cross the inside of the windshield before I happen upon a black cat – which is why it looks like I play tic-tac-toe on my windshield. With all these safety precautions, why won't my other half teach me how to cut metal with his cutting torch?

I mean, years ago I stopped jumping out of my skin when he lit the thing, making it pop and sending these little floating pieces of acetylene through the air. I quit being standoffish about the sparks being thrown in all directions when the steel gave way to the fire. I no longer worry about globs of hot molten iron dropping off the cut and falling onto my foot-because I quit wearing sandals in the shop.

So, what in the world do I have to do to be taught the magic of the cutting torch?

Well, I think I have found the reason. I am what is known as "the ground crew."

This revelation came to me when I recently heard a man telling of his delight in seeing his wife hook up and unhook things he was moving with the aid of the front end loader of a tractor he borrowed. He was in the driver's seat and she was on the ground doing all the grunt work and taking directions from him. He was very pleased with his new role in their relationship. They had never had the use of a tractor in lifting outside stuff and moving one heavy pot to that corner of the backyard and another odd garden doo-hickey to the backyard. He drove and gave instructions with hand signals and whistles, while she fell into the ground-crew role. Just like yours truly did oh-so-many years ago.

Oh, she was being groomed for this role. I am an old hand at it, so I felt it was my duty to clue her in. I took her aside and explained to her just what was happening. See, she was new to this phenomenon and unless she got some intervention, she would soon find herself owning her very own set of knee pads and pairs of lined and unlined leather gloves to fit the season to hook up a chain with one hand and tighten a ratcheting nylon strap with the other, both at the same time. We ground crew are very versatile.

But back to that shiny Victor Journeyman cutting torch with its mighty oxygen and acetylene tanks attached to the torch head by gauges and red and green hoses – one of which is left-hand threaded so as not to get the two mixed up when the ground crew changes out the heavy green-and-black tanks.

Will I ever be shown the ins and outs of getting the blue tip of fire just right? Will I ever have the opportunity to put on a rosebud tip and have more fire than you can shake a stick at? Heating up a piece of iron until it glows rosy red and eye-popping orange?

Truth be told? Probably not.

With beads of sweat on his forehead, my other half says, "You and fire just aren't a good match." Get it? Match…fire. Oh well, I really have no need to bend some ole piece of steel anyway. Besides, I like wearing sandals.

29

Learning, Always Learning
For Jimmy

My dad played the drums, a fact that even my brother didn't know until recently when we were talking about cleaning out junk in our respective houses. Upon mentioning that I still had Dad's drumsticks, my brother had appeared bewildered.

Like my brother, I too had stumbled across the mysterious sticks with my dad while we were cleaning out our old garage — not sure I was actually helping him as I don't really see myself being the kind to spend much time cleaning out garages as a youngster. More to the point, I don't see myself spending much time with my parents; it was more likely he was cleaning the garage and I had just happened by at the time he had withdrawn his sticks from some hidey hole to give them a try.

Okay, now that we have the story straight, here we go…

I asked Dad where they had come from and he had said they were his. No *way*. My dad hip enough to play the drums? No. He was Dad, not Ringo. Yes, Ringo. I am old enough to recall Ringo when he was just Ringo, not *the* Ringo he thinks he is today.

I need to stop with the commentary.

So, I asked Dad to give me a sample of his *pa-rum-a-pum-pum*, thinking he would *rat-a-tat* something like a kid would with a wooden spoon and a floor full of pots and pans. But he shot me a crooked grin and played the sticks on several things in the garage with a masterful hand and a beat that made my toes tap. I was amazed. Then I asked him if he could do a drum roll, the only drum talk I knew at that time. He wailed off a drum roll atop an old plastic hamper. Again, I was amazed. I didn't see it then, but looking back now, I can see that he was living past moments of his life. Like I do. Like many people do, especially around the Fourth of July, when friends and families gather after a year or many years apart, when stories and memories flood the ground around your feet. It's amazing!

In Ely, Nevada, there is what is called an "all-class reunion" over the holiday where graduates of all ages and classes of White Pine High School return home to do what we White Piners do best – enjoy living.

Of course, this is a party atmosphere that is not restricted to just this one Eastern Nevada town. It happens all over the country. I cannot speak of what they do in France or Costa Rica as I am not from France or Costa Rica. But in Nevada, we have reunions with all the trimmings. Food, talk, drink, talk, water fights, talk, dragging Main Street, talk. Seems to be a theme of ole-time fun here. With all that talking, you would think that we would know everything by the time we celebrate like, 20, 30, or more years out of high school. But you would be mistaken.

Just like when I was a fledgling teenager finding out my dad played the drums, I still find out things about school that make me go, "*Really?*" I don't think I am alone in thinking that my class was the best class to come out of that school – uh, the old high school, not the new fancy one that I have never been in. Now *that* makes me feel the tap of years on my shoulders!

Oh, there were classes close to mine that were nearly as good as our class was and I know people from classes above and below me. But what I find hard to take are the classes of 2008, 2009, or 2010 having their ten-year reunions. The class of 1975 is having their 45th reunion. That one I can see, but are there people who have been out of high school for ten and twenty years that actually graduated in the new millennium? That is like meeting someone who was born in 1988. I was out of school for a few more years than I like to admit by 1988.

How are *you* feeling about the years under your belt by now?

I look forward to learning more each time I run into someone whose life intersected with mine. I've reconnected with some great friends over the years and they are amazing people who are treasures to me.

So, to the newly-graduated and to those graduates from less than ten years ago, I say:

"Hang in there. You aren't going to believe what you see in 20 or 30 years whenever you go back to your alma mater. Ask about so-and-so when you run into someone from your past. And do talk about your school years with your kids. Pull out your metaphorical drum sticks and give them a show!"

Trina
WPHS Class of 1973!
Go Bobcats!

30

Cutting My Purse Strings
For Russell

The journey that is taken to accomplish things in life is sometimes poignant or heartbreaking. Sometimes even the smallest of decisions have such an impact that the reverberations are felt for more minutes than Carter's has Little Liver Pills. Well, that should tell you my age. As of early 2020, I am 64, for those interested.

Now, I tell you that number to justify to you, but mostly to validate myself and my avant-garde decision to quit carrying a purse, a satchel, a backpack, or a daily suitcase. This monumental decision was not undertaken lightly. Oh no, my friend. It has been coming for quite some time.

I started to question the whole purse-carrying thing just after I got married. My new husband, so handsome and manly, asked me to carry a little plastic salt shaker filled with something called Lowry's Seasoning Salt, a garlicy spiced-up salt, so he would have it at restaurants because he just love, love, *loved* it on everything. The newness of marriage was upon me, so I agreed to carry this teeny-tiny, designed-for-camping, two-inch-long shaker in my purse.

Oh, and I was to make sure it was full whenever we left on any trip, be it overnight or for an extended vacation. How cute, huh? But a voice in my newlywed head sent a whisper of doubt about the decision to carry this didn't-weigh-more-than-two-ounces do-dah! I should have listened!

That salt shaker opened the zipper to my purse and soon more goodies climbed in! Next it was, "Honey, will you put my wallet, keys, glasses, broken faucet part to be replaced, pair of pliers, and address book in your purse?"

And I did.

Everything that was pre-iPhone ended up in my purse. As a matter of fact, I guess I could be considered as the first iPhone!

As time went by, I found myself carrying not only my phone, but his phone. Not only my stash of gum and breath mints, but his too because he didn't enjoy the flavors I liked. Before I knew it, my little purse that when I was single and carefree had carried a hair brush, chapstick, my driver's license, and a ten-dollar bill had morphed into a hobo bag complete with a red handkerchief tied to the strap in case a grease rag was needed!

Oh, I was at the ready for anything, up to and including a nuclear attack!

Then the tide began to change. We grew our lives together to become one. How romantic it all seems – in the rear view. We built businesses, ran farms, and what now as I remember was my cute hobo bag, became a double-strapped, red, quilted shoulder bag with extra outside pockets for those readily-needed items. You know, glasses, keys, pad and pen, Kleenex, and half-eaten Kleenex lint-laden rolls of Lifesavers. The life essentials. But the bag had become a mobile office too. Papers, files, notebooks, and on and on. But this giant shoulder bag was not big enough yet!

No, no, no!

One year for my birthday, I got what I referred to as "The Moose Bag!" Not just because it had a depiction of a moose handcrafted on the rich, leathery side, but because I felt like a moose carrying all seven pounds of it – and that was when it was empty!

My other half was *so* proud when he gave it to me. Told me all about how he had to walk an extra block to this special store to buy it while we were on vacation in Booth Bay Harbor, Maine. How he had it wrapped and the workout it took for him to walk back to the car carrying my so very wonderful *Moose Bag*! It really was pretty and I did and do appreciate the gift – I'm not one to look a gift-horse, or a gift-moose, in the mouth.

That was the last time he ever carried Mr. Moose!

When The Moose Bag was used in its heyday, it regularly topped out at 40 to 50 pounds laden with papers, lunch, the odd can of spray paint, a half-gallon of milk picked up at the store on the way home, and even one or two small pets.

Oh, and now I was carrying The Moose Bag *and* a purse!

My birthday was in June. By October, I found myself sitting in an orthopedic clinic to get my very first cortisone shot in my Moose Bag-carrying shoulder. What a tangled web we weave when first we practice carrying teeny-tiny salt shakers!

Then something amazing happened.

Retirement!

Hurray, no more Moose Bag.

Pishaw!

Now, the moose bag carried a whole new array of life essentials – maps, picnic supplies, swimsuits, and towels… Finally, after making an appointment for my third Moose-shoulder shot and finding myself seeing Russell, a physician's assistant (a.k.a. "the shooter,") I asked, "Russell, what can I do to help this shoulder? Will it always be a pain?"

Despite Russell being soft-spoken, we had a great laughing time when I went to see him. Sitting on a rolling stool dressed in a white coat and wielding a syringe of the good stuff – sometimes I clapped when he entered the room – he looked at me and said with a grin, "Geeze Trina, stop carrying that 50-pound Moose Bag around, will ya!"

Well. duh!

It was such a lightbulb, cloud-parting, sunshine-in-the-window moment. A true right-of-passage epiphany. Life could be accomplished without carrying everything on your shoulder. Really? Who knew and didn't tell me?

So, off The Moose Bag came.

Sure, it was hard going cold-turkey.

Sure, I walked a bit askew for a while, tipping too far to the right to compensate for the loss of the poundage on my left shoulder. But I did it! It was kinda like quitting smoking. Just do it!

Ah, freedom, relief, liberation!

But there was still my ever-present purse. So, I slowly started to go purse-less a little bit at a time too, choosing to leave it home and carry a few bucks in my pocket instead. I frequently went through it and took more things out with wonderment – just what had I been thinking?

But I still hadn't gone completely purse-less. If we were going on long excursions, I still grabbed the old bag.

That was about to change.

I was in a public restroom in a hospital. It was what you might call a one-holer – just me, the sink, toilet, hand dryer, and not one hook, shelf, or spot to set a purse! So, I set it on the edge of the sink as I proceeded to do what I was in there for. All things were going well as the Diet Coke I drank earlier had overstayed its welcome.

Then, for some mystical reason, all on its own, my purse tipped into the sink – a sink that had an *automatic* on faucet! Yes, the kind that when something is put in front of the faucet, the water starts to flow. To clarify, not only was there water flowing from me, but there was water flowing onto and into my purse in the sink that was just a few, try-to-stretch-without-standing-up inches out of reach! I just sat there, hung my head, and giggled as there was "water, water everywhere, but not a drop able to be stopped!"

So, no more hauling for this salt shaker, man's wallet-carrying, paper-toting, Moose Bag-shoulder shooting, wet-purse-packing woman.

I was like a television commercial – a cute, young woman leaving her apartment with her phone in one pocket and a credit card in the other. I mean, really, what else do you need?

Well, there is one small item I have carried in purses and Moose Bags for more than 30 years that I now carry in my pocket. I found a pretty blue marble in a parking lot one day and, being me, I picked it up and put it in my purse. Ever since, I have told myself that no matter what else happens, when it seems that I may have lost all my marbles, I will still have one – a pretty little blue that I call Baby Blue and she lives in my pocket!

Yes! I call my marble Baby Blue. Hey, I'm a girl and girls reserve the right to name things. Cars, shovels, lawn mowers, my Harley, hair brushes… Oh, such another story for another day.

31

A Box of Rocks
For Merlin

I can still reach my toes in the morning. Might have to coax my back into bending all that way by testing it a few times, but eventually the tips of my fingers and my toes say hi and then they just become distant relatives until the next day. There are more than a few exercise gurus that I spot as I zip through channels on my television while looking for the next mind-numbing program that will cause me to say, yet again, "There is nothing worth watching on any of the zillion channels we get."

You're nodding in agreement, aren't you?

I just can't watch exercise programs. I feel too guilty and silly jumping up and dancing around my living room with someone all fit and trim shouting encouragement at me from their chic one-bedroom studio apartment shrouded in greenery and natural lighting. I'm a far cry from their ideal demographic as the floor squeaks under my feet and the walls shake until pictures of family and friends tumble to the floor.

No, I figure my day is full enough of hither and yon, to and fro, up and down, lift and carry. I don't think I need to add bend and squat to my list. I do, however, still dance in my kitchen in the mornings as I listen to music of the sixties and seventies.

My heart, along with my doctors, medical insurance companies, and now even some government health department minions, seem to be asking me to do extra daily activity to keep that same heart pumping along. Apparently, it has been deemed essential to add exercise to our daily routine. Oh *swell!* Well, if I must choose, I choose walking as my extra daily exercise.

And that is where my box of rocks comes in.

Spring is on the horizon and with winter waning, I have noticed that my frame has an added layer again. I say it was put there just to keep me insulated from the cold; my scale says it was put there because of the coffee-and-chocolate-chip ice cream the Chevron store used to carry along with the fact that I am of the school that says you don't go out and walk in the snow and ice of winter. But to fit into the shorts of summer, the ones hiding and quivering with fear in the back of my closet, I must not dally another day in shedding winter to re-discover that spring in my step.

To that end, as I trudged up the steps to my back door the other day after a long day of bookwork and tax preparation, I found a big ole box of rocks waiting for me. Upon first glance, I decided that they were something my other half had put there to fill in some hole our dogs had dug. Or to put them where the rain gutter gutters the water off the roof and makes a hole in the grass.

Rain gutters are a source of contention that will be discussed later.

But having other after-hours things that needed to be done, I side-stepped the box of rocks and dragged my winter-layered self into the house to make mac and cheese for dinner. Like I really needed any more mac and cheese in my face!

During dinner, my other half asked if I had seen the present he had left for me. Mentally, I scanned the deck and checked off dogs, cats, firewood, cat tree, 48-inch circular saw blade, stuffed mouse, and… what else? *Oh!* The box of rocks.

Imagining the worst, like having to carry them some place and do something with them and hoping the someplace and something is close and easy, I said, "Thanks?"

He replied proudly that he had leveled our graveled yard that morning. See, we live on a five-acre parcel and the yard with mud, rain, and snow tends to get ruddy at which point, my other half turns to the huge railroad tie he fashioned into a drag that he pulls behind the tractor to level the yard to make driving to the house more serene and less like forging a river, climbing the Alps, and crossing the Rio Grande.

So, after the leveling, he spends the next few hours picking up most of the rocks that were bigger than a pack of cigarettes. This particular time, he told me, he had "picked up the ankle getters," the ones I could turn an ankle on when I started my pre-spring daily walking exercise – his oh-so-elegant way of pushing me out the door. Of course, what I heard was: "Come on now, honey. Let's get out there and get going. Spring and summer are just around the corner…"

But he verbalized it loud and clear without opening his mouth; he had just said it by offering a box of rocks!

I could go one of two ways there.

1. I could let my ire get the best of me and think, *Well! He thinks my winter-layered self is unattractive...*
2. Or I could find delight in the fact that he had spent the day picking up rocks, the safety of my ankles foremost on his mind as I got my winter-layered self out there to walk.

The path I chose was…

32

The Notorious Hot vs. Cold Discussion
For John

It is nearly 100 degrees outside which brings up the topic of preferences. Which is better? The heat of summer or the cold of winter? This conversation, I have noticed, has two very distinct sides. Surprisingly, it is not a gender-sided conversation which I find refreshing. It has nothing to do with age, height, weight, hair color, or any number of other things that make us all unique. No, the heat tolerance/cold tolerance line crosses all human boundaries. If you haven't had the opportunity to discuss the preference with those around you, do so at your own peril. The likelihood of there being a complete difference of opinion is 100 percent. Guaranteed.

Let us first consider summer and all its sun and flowers and outside activities. Summer, when you don't have to wear several layers of clothes so you don't freeze as you thaw your car in the morning. Summer, when the grass is green, even on the far, far side of the hill, everything blooms wreaking havoc on those who suffer from allergies, and sweat runs off the tip of your nose.

And... winter, with the beautiful snow-covered mountains and cool crisp air. Winter with activities like sledding, skiing, and snowmobiling. Winter, when you get to buy that new coat or cozy up to a nice fire – both of which are activities that you do to keep, uh, warm! And it is not sweat but another type of liquid that runs out from the inside of your nose because it is so cold outside.

I am a summer person.

Now you know which side of the line I stand on. I don't enjoy being so hot that I get testy. However, I don't think there are too many of the winter people that think getting so cold everything hurts is desirable either. No matter where you stand, there seems to be two sides to this conversation. For example:

We summer-timers say the heating bills are less in summer. Those winter-timers come back with the fact that the water bills in summer to keep grass green are atrocious.

Winter-timers like to bundle up and enjoy the feel of wool against their skin. Summer-timers say throw on a pair of shorts and t-shirt and get outside and enjoy the summer. We like the feel of cotton on our skin.

Winter-timers are the ones who crazily play hooky-bob on the back of a passing car, slip-sliding like an ice cube across a linoleum floor, or racing down a snow-covered mountain on a pair of sticks – or even one wide stick!

Summer-timers run through lawn sprinklers as they dot the landscape with ice-cold droplets of water. Or going for a long hike up the aforementioned mountain just to see what they can see. Summer-timers do this without fear of broken legs, arms, or other appendages because it's summer!

My affinity for summer can be reduced to this though – stripping out of clothes to keep cool is easier than layering bulky sweaters and jackets on until you are so bundled up that if you fell over, you wouldn't be able to get up without the assistance of a passing crane. And the chances of you falling in the path of a passing crane are pretty slim.

Speaking of slim, let me start my ending with the biggest problem some have with summer – the swimsuit. I know that I do not have a swimsuit body, but I'm okay with that. Finally! Only took a few blah-blah years, but I'm there. I can still hear my high school sewing teacher telling us girls – yes girls, because boys didn't take sewing classes way back in the Stone Age when I went to school – "Don't hide inside big coats or sweaters. You are what you are and that's all there is to it. Revel in your own uniqueness."

And that is just what I do every summer, shorts and t-shirts galore.

Oh, and let us not even get into the thermostat dispute. Up, down, up, down. Thankfully someone did come up with a dual-controlled electric blanket as well as a personal handheld fan that is attached to a spritzing water bottle.

Of course, such conversations regarding preferences leads us to the discussion of which is better – spring or fall?

I like spring, he likes fall.

Imagine that!

33

The Fingers of Life

For Julie

In my everyday life, I try to stay away from the lumping syndrome. Lumping is the practice of using words like everybody, nobody, every time, or I *absolutely guarantee*. For instance, "I never get to go anywhere!" "Everybody else has one!" "I guarantee you'll like it." Mothers on the block where I grew up with their years of knowledge and experience of handling these situations, were famous for their replies to a lumping accusation from a distraught teenager.

"If *everybody* jumped off a bridge, would you jump too?"

Although I try not to lump, I humbly guarantee that after reading the following, you will never look at your hand, be it right or left, the same way again.

So, take a quick glance at your hand, the five-fingered miracle. I want to focus on those digits first. I have found a profound correlation between people and each finger. Let's take a closer look.

Out on the end, I give you the little finger, the pinky. I know people who are like the pinky. Small, petite, proportioned, and nearly perfect. Just as the pinky is poised delicately high and is very noticeable when drinking from a dainty tea cup, pinky people have a need to be noticed. In some cases, they should be. To some extent their daintiness is natural, inherited, a product of generations of slender genes. There is, unfortunately, a tendency for the non-pinky types to try to be pinkies and that is just unattractive. For goodness sake, if you're not a pinky, don't wear pinky clothes or do pinky-style dancing. Just be happy with your non-pinky self and go about your non-pinky life. However, *beware*. I've noticed that my pinky grows a wicked nail that can scratch at the least little provocation. Pinkies have power that can be used for good or evil.

Moving to the right, or left if you have chosen to study your right hand, we have the finger commonly known as "the ring finger." Society has, in some ways, made this finger look like an unfinished finger without some sort of adornment. Maybe you know a ring-finger person. A ring-finger can become a bling-adorned person, an individual who loves lots of bling in their lives. One who will and often does nearly anything to catch your eye as you pass. A blinger will wear lots of fashion attire, great jewelry, or make-up. Maybe (s)he wears a hat, but doesn't have a hat-friendly face. The blingers I know just want to be part of a circle. Watch for those who overdo it in your everyday life. Stop and give them an extra bit of your time. Like the ring finger though, remember a little bit of bling goes a long way.

Now the one you've been waiting for! The middle finger, the center of the hand – dare I say? – the bird. This strong, self-centered digit is high and above the rest. It can, without any help from anyone, stand alone! In standing alone, it can make a strong, to-the-point statement without much effort. The middle-fingered person has a tendency to overpower, bully, or bulldoze. But realize this, my friends, when you are outnumbered, out-gunned, or out of your league, you want a middle finger on hand – *pun intended!* – to help you through the tough times!

What is there to say about the next digit? The pointer of the bunch. The helpful index finger, the quiet, unobtrusive one that, by chance of position, quickly and aptly hits more keys on a keyboard. Thus, the pointer does more work on that keyboard and in life than any other finger. Single-fingered, if you will… The pointer, the one that can "pick" – *yuck!* – out things in your life that would be better off left alone. The finger that hails to millions of sports fans in huge foam forms that they are number one! This little sport feels uncomfortable adorned with bling but will be the first one you see when you shake hands, making it honest and dependable. This little friend comes into your life and does its job without complaining.

This helpful Hannah helps you hold on to things with the help of a neighboring friend, the thumb.

Ah yes, the thumb. The last member of the five pack that pulls all the others together. The thumb is short and squat. The pinkies like the thumbs' short squatness; it makes them feel good inside. Blingers know that you can try to add bling to the thumb, and some do it nicely, but in reality, the thumb doesn't need bling. In regard to the middle finger, the thumb can stand alone and make its own statement – "Hey, I need a ride! I need some help! Can you give me a hand?"

Or the thumb can give the universal "All's good" symbol – thumbs up! Or a not so-good thumbs down. The thumb is the only finger that can reach all the other fingers by itself. It is strong and it is the first thing you see when you give or get a gift, be it money, a letter, or a helping hand. Wow, to be a thumb in life.

Holding your hand together is the palm. Psychics say your life line is in the palm of your hand. I like to think of my palm as the key to my life. I can close my fingers around my palm as I bring those around me close when I need them. Just glance around at your handy family, friends, and acquaintances. Inside I am, and always will be, a pinky even though my outsides look rather thumb-ish. I have a sister-in-law who is bling-ish, but she does it so well that she wouldn't be herself if she changed. I wish I had some of her "bling-ish-ness." I have friends I know I can count on to stand up with me and protect me if I ever need it. Before my other half moved to heaven, he did more quiet work in ten minutes than I could in a whole day and he did a lot of it just for me. He was my number one.

I hope when you look at your hand and palm, that you can see your family, friends, and the future of your life.

A wave takes on a grand new meaning when you look at your hand in this way. As does a pat on the back for a job well done or a warm palm on your shoulder as you embrace a loved one. What a great feeling that is.

When you get one of those dang paper cuts, or you have more than a little trouble opening that bag of chips, or your hands are dry and just seem to hurt, perhaps there is someone in your fingers of life that is in need of some attention.

34

A Wrinkling of Your Nose
For Nancy P

Hear ye, hear ye!

I think we need a decree that creates a universally accepted gesture to signal the presence of bad breath.

It is a touchy subject, a very personal but public thing that we have all had and have unleashed upon the world. Or have had forced upon our sense of smell at one time or another by what I am sure were unknowing individuals who had the pizza with extra pepperoni and onions. You are exuberantly nodding, aren't you?

Do you think it is worse to have bad breath or to be on the receiving end of it? Neither is optimal, but what exactly is the best method to deal with someone who has eaten week-old roadkill?

Unless you are a hermit, you get a lot of air spilled your way daily by talking to other humans. It would be such a relief to be able to make a gesture everyone knew to subtly let your conversational mate know that they need a mint, gum, or jack hammer and a pick to remove whatever is causing the sour air that is curling your eyebrow hairs. I have learned that when someone offers me a piece of gum or a Tic Tac, they might be trying to tell me something. So, with that in mind, I always accept the offer with a smile. Conversely, I have tried to offer gum to a few foul air makers. Some accept, thankfully.

But what do you do with the ones who decline your offer? Is it then time to say, "Hey, your garlic bread and spaghetti from last night has followed you to a new day?" Is that too subtle?

You could say, "Excuse me while I go to the eye doctor to see if he can fix my eyes; your breath seems to have melted them." That might be too far the other way.

In the movie *The Sting*, the grifters would swipe the side of their nose with a finger toward each other to signal their acknowledgment of a piece of information. So that method is out. You touched your nose, didn't you? Me too. Sam Spade would run his hand along the brim of his hat to get a dame's attention, but I don't know many people who sport a felt fedora, so that too is out.

After much – okay, maybe a bit *too much* – thought, I deem that we wrinkle our noses during conversations to signal, "*Pee-ew!* Bud, you need a trip to the mouthwash bottle and the spit sink." From this day forward that could be the official "signal" telling you that you are belting out a green cloud.

But you have to pay attention to the face!

Is it smiling? Turning blue with asphyxiation? Or did you see the nose wrinkle, just a touch? Maybe wrinkle twice, or thrice, or…

Let's face it, there really is no easy way to handle this. The direct approach, as in many things in life, would be the best. But let's just say you're talking to someone and they wrinkle their nose. Just a slight wrinkle. I mean, come on! Let's not look like we are a herd of rabbits. It could work! Try it in front of a mirror.

Yes, I tried it before writing this little do-dah to see if it could be done discretely.

It can.

Actually, it's kinda cute – in a bunny kind of way.

35

Chocolate-Covered Bacon

For Roy

I thought about keeping you on the edge of your seat before I named the dish my husband wanted to make and take to a potluck/surprise baby shower we attended. But there is no way to fit chocolate-covered bacon into a little story without just coming out and saying we took as a side dish chocolate-covered bacon.

Now, upon first hearing about this recipe my other half had come across on the internet, I wanted to take his laptop away from him. His intentions were good, but chocolate-covered bacon just sounded like a waste of two really great ingredients – chocolate and bacon. But I have found that if I just go with the flow instead of trying to swim against the current, we are both happier.

So, he printed the recipe off the internet and I read it and he read it – well, I assumed he read it – and off to the store we went to get the ingredients. I knew we were in trouble when we didn't agree on the amount of this epicurean delight we would be making; in other words, we couldn't agree on how much chocolate and bacon we needed to purchase! Not to mention what *type* of the two ingredients.

We have had the most civilized discussions – yes, sometimes teeth-clenched discussions – in stores. I huff; he puffs. Over years and years and years of huffing and puffing, I have found that since I am always right, it is best if I just let him have his way and then do it my way later. Such was the case here.

Long ole story short, we got home with the bacon and chocolate and at the appointed time, he fried the quarter strips to a lovely crisp, after which he realized that I had been right and that the recipe had called for quarter strips, *not* strips cut into sixths. But why split hairs now, right?

I must say, he is the best bacon fryer. He has the patience to let it fry unadulterated. I, on the other hand, do not and so, after too much heat, the wrong size pan, and not enough patience, I end up with bacon that is more or less a pig in a poke. You know… it looks like bacon, smells like bacon, but is either too crisp and burnt or not done enough and has that chewy, fatty squishy texture – I saw that face you just made!

Anyway, with the bacon done, I proceeded to melt the dark and milk chocolates. *Yum*. In another jury-rigged double boiler, I melted what was supposed to be white chocolate but had ended up as candy with little pieces of cookie mixed in. Oh well, it was just for decoration anyway – the instructions directed us to pull a wire whisk through the melted white chocolate and shake it over the already dark chocolate-dipped pieces for an added "ta-da" factor. You know, like topping a baked potato already slathered in butter with a dollop of sour cream and then chives and pepper. Maybe some cheese or bacon or chili… Some cooks just don't know when to stop. But off I go on another foolish food rant.

After the bacon cooled, the chocolate-dipping began.

Should we use little tongs to dip?

Maybe put a toothpick into each little bacon tidbit?

We opted for the hand-dipped method. Cleaning all matter off the counter, with gloved hands the drowning began. I have to tell you that I was more than a little sad at the sight of two pounds of quarter-sliced bacon strips being half-covered with the mixture of dark and milk chocolate. I really like bacon, as I think most people do.

I should say that I understand why some people are vegetarians, but in reality, I don't. Come on – its *bacon*! It's one of the biggest reasons we have thumbs!

After refrigeration, we had a huge cookie sheet covered in foil with, like, 60 little squiggly hard-shelled bits of… Well, let me just say that you have got to try them! They are unbelievable.

As word of the new dish spread at the party, I heard one man, as he chewed a piece, declare, "Here comes the bacon flavor!" Another partygoer passing by, pointed and said, "Now that is just wrong." And then he took a piece… or was it two or three? Another advised that he thought the tidbits should be their own food group.

So, kudos to the man in my life who was brave enough to try something new.

But ladies, don't ever let them know that they have the upper hand. You'll never get it back. And maybe that's okay. Fifty-fifty isn't a bad thing, is it?

Email me for the recipe!

Oh and by the way, the baby was a cutie. Her name is Clementina. I love that name. However, if the happy mom had named her Clemen*trina* I would not have objected. Oh, they were so close! HAHAHAHA

36

Fibber Drawers

For Eva

Back in the 1940s and 50s, many families gathered around the radio after supper at 8 p.m. without fail to listen together to a radio show called "Fibber McGee and Molly."

Finally, something before *my* time!

The hook to the show was when Fibber McGee went to the hall closet to find something. He would swing the door open with a creak and a thunderous commotion of clangs, twangs, and crashes would follow as mountains of stuff fell out on top of him. Those mountains had been oh-so-lovingly and carefully put in the closet by Molly. As time marched on, family radio time was replaced with the wonderful invention of television. That closet may have faded away, but it was replaced by the "Fibber Drawer."

Yes, a Fibber Drawer. In most homes, it is usually an unintentionally chosen drawer in the kitchen. You can pick it out because it has the stickiest handle, sometimes doesn't shut all the way, and is filled with the things that need to be within arm's reach in case of a nuclear disaster. Such important things like – well, you know:

notebooks with all the pages written on
lighters that might light one more time if you hold them at an angle
long-forgotten stray packages of gum and mints
old ketchup and mustard packets
rubber cement
thumbtacks
rubber gloves
a TV guide from five years ago
a piece of string or some of those plastic bread wrapper closers

an ashtray pilfered from Harrah's Club in Reno
some broken pencils and dried-up markers…

Oh, my friends, the list goes on and on. What should
not go on and on, but admittedly does in our home, is the fact
that our house has grown more than one Fibber Drawer!

There seems to be different degrees of Fibber
Drawers too. There are drawers that start out to be
specifically designated for things like, say, cookbooks. Then,
in just the blink of an eye, in some magical way, that
cookbook drawer is filled with old sunglasses, more dried-up
pens and pencils without erasers, a back scratcher, et cetera,
et cetera. How in the world does that happen?

So, I thought it might be a good idea to set a trap for
our wayward Fibber Drawer creator because there is
absolutely *no way* on God's green Earth that I have created
this Fibber Drawer in *my* kitchen. Okay. So here was the plan.

First, I thought I would empty an entire drawer in the
kitchen, one close to the phone (or where the phone used to
be and now is just an empty place to sit and ponder what I
went into the kitchen for). Near this drawer where the phone
once was is a cup full of pens and pencils and a stack of those
sticky note pads of which you need to thumb through to find
a sheet that does not already have some sort of note written
on it.

Note: said supplies are on the counter because there is no room in
the drawer where they should be!

After emptying the drawer of its contents, I would
leave it open just a touch to entice and beckon all those
Fibber Drawer adders. Next, I… Oh, come on! Who am I
kidding? You too see the problem with this plan, right?

Clean out an entire drawer in the kitchen?

Oh please! Just what should I do with those most
important items I would take out? Where would the three-
year-old phone books go? What about the little plastic dump

truck which carries those colorful rubber pencil-top erasers that rolls back and forth when I open and close that drawer?

Every plan has some sort of flaw. But I didn't think the first item on the list would be such a *fatal* flaw. Clean out a drawer... Ha!

Just what do we do when all the drawers in the kitchen fill up? Well, for goodness sake, we move on into the bedroom to the nightstands of course. In our house, to get to the bedroom you have to pass by the hall closet. Please, don't ask! Suffice it to say the hall closet is *not* where we keep our coats.

Ah, the meat of the bone – or the bone of contention. The nightstand drawers are truly where this all began. I went looking for cough drops. Easy enough, right? Does it not make sense that cough drops should be in the nightstand? Don't you need cough drops in the night when a coughing spell might wake you from what should be a peaceful slumber? You would think so.

I opened the top drawer of my nightstand and there they were. Sitting pretty just waiting for me – three old remote controls from TVs we no longer owned. Next to them a collection of three pens and eight pencils, some still complete with the colored rubber toppers.

Going through a Fibber Drawer is like mining. Sometimes you find gold in them-thar drawers, but mostly you need a pick and shovel to get to the bottom.

So, come on now.

Fess up.

Just how many Fibber Drawers do you have in your house?

37

A Huge Power Surge
For Don

Yes, we all bemoan the electronic world and the bumps and bruises it occasionally inflicts on us. I actually try my level best not to generalize like that by saying, "We all." But I have yet to meet someone who does not have some horror story about the delicate balance between adding content, saving, and then hitting print.

It's gotten to the point now that when I hit print, I drop to my knees with my head bowed and cross myself. As an extra measure, I cross all my fingers and toes! Well, as it sometimes happens, even my finger and toe crossings don't help.

On one particular day as the printer blinked its orange WIFI wiper blade at me, I knew I had been defeated.

Of course, I am not without some computer knowledge. I can find my control panel and I can even open the printer icon thingy. From there, I can read all about the bytes being sent to and from, the properties of my under-75-dollar printer, and even who my printer likes to date on Saturday nights. FYI: he likes to see the digital camera sitting next to him all dolled up in her come-hither black case! I can see everything except what to do to make that orange light turn to green.

But like so many of these stories, nothing ever goes smoothly. This all started a week or so prior to the orange-light event when our house was hit by lightning. We fared well, no fire, no hole in the roof, no flying witches on bicycles. Apparently, the bolt of electricity flew around in the air, looked our house over, and – *zap, crack, bang!* – picked the internet radio antenna as its entry way into our home. You see, we live on a spot on Mother Earth that attracts these wayward bolts of lightning as our five acres has been hit several times in the past 40 years. So, you would think we would have either moved by now or gotten used to the torment that comes with the frequent inclement weather. Well, we haven't done either.

We placed some nine or ten different items on our list of things to replace since the surge protection devices we have are only equipped to handle the occasional power surge from the power company. Maybe even a surge from a distant lightning strike. You know, when you see a flash and then count – one Mississippi, two Mississippi, three Mississippi…Then the number at which you hear the roll of the thunder is how many miles away the lighting is. Yeah, those far away lightning strike power surges are what surge protectors are built for.

Now back to your regularly scheduled programming…

We ordered new televisions and got a new DVD player. We even had a great guy come out and get our internet back up and running. However, I will be calling him again!

See, the printer worked the morning after the storm, but when he left our house after two or three hours of grumble, mumble, and an occasional, "Well, what the…" under his breath, the printer decided it was on strike. I know the internet has nothing to do with the printer, but this great internet guy will surely take pity on this frazzled housewife and come back and do magic to get the thing going again. I hope – again, with all my fingers and toes crossed.

Oh, and the icing on the cake of this little lightning strike?

The death of my heating pad.

Yes, it has gone into the great beyond of small electrical appliances. Now on the surface, this may seem quite petty, considering all the terrible things that could have happened with a huge bolt of lightning coming into a home. But this particular heating pad was very old and durable. The best thing about it was that it *didn't* have an automatic timer that turned off the heating pad every two hours. Who in the world thought that would be a good idea?

My old pad was turned on at bedtime and unceremoniously stuffed at the bottom of my bed under my feet. In the mornings, I still had warm tootsies and the cat liked it too. Now, with a new-fangled "safer" heating pad, my nights will never be the same. Even the cat is upset. If I wasn't so electronically-challenged, I bet I could break into that new heating pad and disable its timer-thingy.

Yeah, and I could get the printer printing too. Yeah, yeah. Sure. Sure, Trina.

The only thing that stayed a constant in this whole unfortunate list of problems was the two huge owls in the trees outside of our house. They continued to hoot and screech into the nights and the still early mornings. Never missing a beat. They were there before the bolt of lightning and are still hootin'.

I mention this because I always heard that having owls around was supposed to be a sign of good luck. Well, I submit that they are not doing their jobs very well.

So, if anyone has any ideas of how to get a printer to stop winking at me, let me know. If not, I guess I could use it as target practice!

Gee, isn't life a hoot and a half?

38

A Barrel of Crackers

For Kamala

I try my best to let gossip pass through my delicate little ears without stopping. I want to know if someone is sick or going through a rough time so that I might be able to do something to help though. Send a card, make a casserole… But to whisper and cackle while taking pleasure in the life circumstances of another person, well, that just doesn't appeal to me. To be honest – of course I am going to be honest – when I was younger, I did tend to be a host car on the gossip train. But, as I assume always happens, the gossip eventually turned onto me. Well, I learned real fast, faster than any guilt trip put on me by a preacher, to be the end-of-the-line person with gossip.

Just what is it about gossip that tantalizes and seduces? Where is the best place to hear gossip? What is the best way to pull up on the reigns and put a sudden "whoa" to a story? Let's start with trying to stop that train.

Why spend your mouth time gossiping when it could be put too better use doing what it is meant for – eating. How intriguing would it be if instead of asking tantalizing questions about a story you're being told to by a gossip that is just on the edge of her seat waiting for your questions so she can continue taking her ride on the back of someone else's misfortune, you stuffed a cracker in your mouth causing a lack of ability to talk, because we all know that it is not polite to talk with your mouth full? *Whew!*

People who can't look away when they go by an accident are the same ones who are most likely to gossip. Their nose is more pronounced than their common courtesy. They are tantalized with those scenes and seduced by bits of half-truths. There is a reason for a fence and reason for open ground. A gossip tells stories over the fence while a true friend has open ground all around themselves.

What about going to the horse's mouth about a story you have just heard from someone that I would call the other end of the horse? Face it head-on. Being the talk of the town is only a good thing if you're rich, famous, and wanting the attention to become richer and famous-er?

In us regular folks' circles, being a gossip with lips of crimson bleeding nonsense isn't all it's cracked up to be. I want to know if the cackle is about me so I may either let it run off me like water off a duck's back, or go to the engineer of the train and ask, "To what end did you begin that story?" Can you just see the terror in the eyes of the "mouth bully" when you step up to the plate and ask that question? Talk about the power of words!

I don't, like my mother did, go to have my hair cut, curled, blown, and shellacked each week (you could have bounced a quarter off her hair!) at the local gossip shop – the hair salon. I go maybe once a year to a gal about 250 miles away from where I live just to give myself a treat.

Oh my, to sit in an atmosphere where you don't know anyone is quite an eye opener. I tell you that to give you something to think about next time you are in public gabbing about him and her, or her and him, or them... I don't know anyone in that salon except the gal doing my hair and I can tell by the pssst, blabbity, and yaddity that goes on there which ones would keep the train going and which would be eating a cracker if they had one.

Imagine you're approached by Ole Gossipy Gert. Here is what you can do: give her a copy of this column with a stack of crackers, smile, and whistle a tune as you walk away. Maybe you won't stop the train permanently, but I bet you a nickel you put a hitch in her get-along.

39

Can and Can't Friends

For Marcia

I can't strike a match on the back of the thigh of my Levis or light one with my thumbnail. I can't spit, not a drop or a pit or a watermelon seed without needing a drool bucket. I can't saw a straight line with a hand saw. I can't even make a good-to-the-last-drop pot of coffee. My I-Can't List is long and actually quite impressive. With all the wonderful things I can't do, how in the world, of the green, green grass of home have I been able to reach my age – of maturity?

Take the spitting for instance. Over the years, my husband gave it the old college try in trying to teach me to spit. He was an outstanding spitter as I have noticed most guys are. Not that he did it regularly, but if push ever came to shove, he could spit with the best of them. Calmly, he showed me how to hold watermelon seeds in my mouth and then how – with magic? – I was to force air out with the seed thereby causing it to fly into the atmosphere with such an arc that a fully-realized rainbow would blush with brighter colors.

So, I held the seed on the inside of my lips, got a burst of air ready to let 'er go, then with all the finesse of a teething, slobbering baby, sent out a deluge of air and spit liquid. After the rain shower stopped, the seed dropped on the ground in front of me no further than the blades of grass on my shoe. Sometimes it just stuck to my chin. So, when I say I can't spit, I say with pride –

I can't spit – really, really well.

It's important to know that there will always be can and can't friends in life. Just like my spitting ability, I know a lady who can't throw a ball. Not that she throws like a girl, mind you, but that she can't throw a ball, *at all*. When she is asked to toss something, those of us who know her automatically duck. From past experiences we've learned that the object in flight will not land where she intended it to. That ability, or lack thereof, is on her Can't List. But it's endearing! Also, she might be unable to properly direct the trajectory of an object in flight, but give her a needle and she can sew you a new pair of pockets in your overalls!

On the other hand – holler if you know this person – there are people within your life travels who tout they can do everything. Climb a mountain, forge a river, and split an atom? Maybe even spit like a pro? Why is it that an I-can-do-it-all attitude is so important? I get the insecurity of wanting to fit in. I even get the notion that knowledge is power. But too much power, like too much garlic, puts people off. Makes them take a step back and say, "Whew!" It's the old, been-there, done-that thing.

I am very happy to know people who *can do* things. But there is a line between knowing something and knowing everything. I have a bag of go-to people in my life who can do great things. And in the course of living, I call on them. I have a Physicians' Assistant friend who can answer my middle-of-the-night medical questions. He also knows cars, but I bet he can't bake a cake and decorate it to look like Mickey Mouse like I can.

I know a great plumber who will help me if I need it, but I bet he can't do a French braid like the braids I can. Actually, maybe he can; he used to "do" hair. But I bet he can't whip up a quart of Roquefort dressing from scratch like me.

When you meet someone who can't do something, it is a whole new ballgame. I like to know you can't lift 200 pounds; neither can I. Huh, we have something in common. I admire that you tell me you can't make a great cup of hot cocoa; I can't make toast without burning the edges. We are *simpatico*. Toast and hot cocoa go together like cat and nip. Just ask my nieces and nephew!

So, let's get out there and be the kind of "can't" friends we need.

40

Elevator Exercising

For Tim

Some things happen out of the blue that make me giggle. While visiting a local hospital, I found myself riding in elevators by myself four or five times a day for several days at a time. It was in a hospital where there were loads of elevators, so many so, that riding alone happened nearly every time on my trips to the fifth floor and back down.

Once I got on an elevator, I moved to the back out of habit. As the big, silver monster started its downward descent, my anxiety swelled and I took a step or two forward. But there's not much room in an elevator to pace, you know. Well, I took those few steps and the most surreal feeling struck me. It was like I was falling through space.

Uh, no! There was no beer involved here.

Apparently, the elevator went down faster than my foot, and as it did, my foot took just the tiniest bit more time to hit the floor. It was like, well, just for a split second, it was like being weightless – something, I might add, I have always wanted to be.

Oh, you have *got* to try this. The next ride down, I tried a few more steps and then I walked in a circle a few times. That felt like I was not only going down a circular staircase, but doing so at more than my regular clippity-clop speed. It was kind of refreshing, giving my legs and brain something to sort out. But then I tried it on an up trip.

Oh, I should have stuck with just enjoying the down trip. If down is like an exhale, up is like an inhale, more of a workout. As the elevator ascended, I raised my foot and then put it back down. The floor of the elevator came up to meet my foot making it feel like I was climbing stairs. It was a remarkable phenomenon too, but not as cool as that fun, freefall on the down ride.

I now find myself doing these exercises every time I am in an elevator – alone. Don't do this with other elevator riders onboard, especially in a hospital where the men in white coats can meet you as the door to the elevator opens. They will escort you to a nice quiet room with padded walls and no windows… or so I've heard.

But talk about being a multitasker! Now, even though I took the elevator, I took the stairs too. I know, I know – it's just a few steps. But I tell myself that a few here and there will add up over time.

There are those of us who listen intently but then strong as the desire is, we just don't do those lovingly doctor-ordered loads of exercises. Oh, we all anticipate doing them and eating right and getting enough sleep, etc. As we all should. However, between that little room in which we get "the talk" and the safety of our car – well, you know what happens. If there is even the slightest breeze in the parking lot, the doctor's words are blown out of my head. My father would say that is because there is not much between my ears to hold stuff in. Funny that I remember that though!

So, these elevator exercises are a step in the right direction. I figure a step here and a step there is better than no step anywhere. I once heard Joan Rivers say that the best exercise for her was a good brisk sit! But that kind of one-two-one-two calisthenics will not help to relieve anyone's muffin top or those lovely love handles.

Keep on stepping.

You'll never get anywhere just standing there!

41

Ice and Age
For Linda

One morning after spending some cold, minus-ten-degrees weather hours feeding the animals and doing chores, I happened to catch a glimpse of my pre-dawn bundled self as I passed a mirror. Of course, I had to wait until my glasses de-fogged to get the full effect, but wow, what a looker! *Oh baby!* I bet the cats and dogs were still laughing outside.

My raggedy, holey, used-to-be-red-but-is-now-faded-to-a-burnt-umber hoodie was pulled taut around my body, its hood cinched under my chin. The worn and pulled from overuse, 100-percent acrylic scarf I had snagged from the coat hanger was also wrapped about my neck and knotted under my chin. *Good thing I have two chins!* I thought to myself – inner crying. I was adorned with deerskin gloves, sweat pants, and old sheepskin-covered slippers with rubber soles that had seen better days.

But you know what? I was not a bit cold. I was comfortable. Of course, my nose, the only piece of flesh exposed to the frigid morning air, was running faster than I could sniffle. But that is neither here nor there.

Oh, what price we pay to look good. I'm not talking about getting your hair done, or nails done, or face done, or something done to any other part of your body to look good. No, this is more along the lines of looking good when you are out and about when it is cold. Here is what I've learned and would like to pass along to save you from your next battle with the cold.

They Call Me Weener!

When you are young, there is this perception of appearance. Now, don't get me wrong. We all want to look our best no matter our age and that is not a bad thing. But if that look gets in the way of comfort, well, I vote for comfort. Yes, when it comes down to a vote, it's comfort: one, appearance: zero. But that comfort vote did not come overnight. There have been more times than not that I have frozen my you-know-what off for the sake of vanity. But no more.

It used to be that when the need arose to go outside to, say, chop ice off water troughs for animals, or maybe something more fun like cutting the annual Christmas tree, I would put on my cute coat with the pretty quilted lining and adorn my head with a festive matching hat and some little mittens that were part of the ensemble.

Sound familiar?

Not to guys, I bet. They just throw on a hat and vest and go. But they have a tendency to try to look rough and tough, wearing a lightweight shirt and the same mesh-backed cap they wear year-round and maybe, just maybe, some cotton gloves. Guys never let it show that they get cold, you know.

More often than not, both the male and female of the species are lucky to make it through those "foo-foo," formative years without something on their body turning black and mushy from frostbite. Yum!

Seriously, what would you rather do if you absolutely have to go out in the cold to blow snow on a bitter winter day? Look good to for the cows, horses, dogs, and sagebrush? Or be warm and toasty and not feel like you have to, well, let's get real here, have to use the bathroom every time the wind blows because you are so cold.

We all know, no matter how old you are, when you are cold, you have to, you know, *go*! I would have so appreciated it if some old lady had told me long ago that comfort and warmth are way better than doing the I-gotta-go dance because I was trying to look good while freezing the end of my nose off.

Enough of why we freeze, let's look at how to fix it. How to be warm as toast when even the mercury in the thermometer won't come out of its hidey hole. When it is so cold the sun looks blue through a frozen haze and pogonip covers the land. That, my friends, is cold.

You need to ditch the thought that everyone is looking at you. You are not going outside in mid-winter to win a fashion show. You are going out to work, probably hard. So, wear layers and a good winter coat and that scarf that has been pushed to the back of the hall closet because it didn't go with anything else. Wear a hat or a hoodie and put the hood up. And tie it too. You lose a lot of heat out the top of your head. Where do you suppose that term "hot-headed" comes from?

42

Crazy YouTube Mechanic
For Rod

I changed the oil in my yellow 1991 Chevy Tracker. After being the "helper bee" for the past 42 years, it was time for me to step up to the plate and give this a go by myself. I had no doubt I could do it. No doubt I wouldn't run over myself. And no doubt that if I messed up, some kind person would fix my screw up. With those no-doubts urging me on, I headed out one bright morning to get to it. Now, don't get ahead of me here…

I won't bore you with all the tiny details of my adventure. But – yes, an oily "but" – maybe I'll share just this one tiny detail.

After I got the plug out, I drained the oil from the oil pan and returned the plug to its rightful place – it was very straightforward. I crawled out from under the little buggy and got back upright, something that seems to take a stitch longer as the seasons come and go. Then I needed to stop and let the world catch up with my eyes as I sat up. When did that start happening?

The filter was next. Luckily, it was easy to get to from the top; all I needed was the filter wrench – yes, I know what a filter wrench is. But *where* the filter wrench was, that was the question. I knew I had gotten it out of the tool box and brought it over to where I was "working." It had been there when I had climbed under the car, but gremlins had apparently taken it as I was mechanic-ing.

Looking around, I inched the full drain pan over with my foot to be sure it was under the filter to catch oil when, and if, I ever got it off. Then I saw a little glint floating in the oil in the pan. Yes, it was the filter wrench. I can't be the only one this has happened to.

After cleaning the wrench with solvent, the rest of the oil change was a piece of cake. I patted myself on the back, because there was not another soul around for me to crow to. I then had to figure out how to get oily hand prints off of the back of my shirt. Admittedly, I contemplated leaving them on there – like the mark of Zorro, but with hands. And oil.

Truthfully, it was a big step for me to do this by myself. The first time I was allowed to "help" many, many moons ago, I poured the oil into the oil filler-thingy with the finesse of a three-year-old tyke sitting in the middle of the kitchen floor pouring orange juice from a full-gallon jug into a four-ounce paper cup. This time, I used a funnel. Live and learn, right? Now that I had mastered the oil change, I moved on like I had a Mister, uh, Miss Good Wrench diploma framed and hung on my shop wall.

My Chevy Truck was showing a light on the dash. That kinda sounds like a good opening line for a joke, doesn't it?

Anyway, this light had been on for a while. After hand wringing and bemoaning here and there, I got instructions from a great guy in my circle of friends that had taken me on as the poor ole widow lady! Yes, I do sometimes play the poor-ole-widow-lady card! HAHAHAHAHAHA

My friend told me about getting a computer reader to find out why the light was on. Which I did. I take instructions well – if I want to. *Wink, wink.* The reader was kind of cool. It wasn't telling me how to change the oil; been there, done that. No, upon reviewing the read out and deciphering the information via the internet, I discovered the mass air flow sensor needed to be changed.

Hey, I changed oil! I am invincible now. But I still didn't know how to do it, so I turned to another very trusted friend – YouTube. If you don't know how to do something, check YouTube! It's amazing what you can learn there. First, I learned how to clean the sensor – *don't* clean the sensor. That doesn't work. In fact, while trying to clean the mass air flow sensor indicator, I had to ask my neighbor to help me. I think he felt sorry for me. He saw me, my truck parked in front of the garage with the hood up, and a *huge* red question mark over my head. So, he meandered over.

After I went through getting the computer-reading thingy, discovered the problem, got the spray stuff used to clean the mass air flow sensors, and found the mass air flow sensor under the hood, my neighbor beebopped over to look at the tools, rags, cleaners, and dirt on my face. Eventually, he muttered, "Crazy YouTube Mechanic."

Yep, that's me. A YouTube mechanic. After years of ordering everything, from a number-60 roller chain with connecting and master links to truckloads of 4-inch, 20-foot lengths of PVC sewer pipe with belled ends, ordering a new part for the truck from Rock Auto online was a cinch.

And now that there's a brand-new mass air flow sensor in a box on the back seat of the truck? I'll be out in the driveway soon, hood up on my truck, a *huge* red question mark floating over my head as I wait for my neighbor to spot me.

Yes, he'll come over.

What a guy!

43

Lime-Green Writing Sticks
For Nancy M.

It's a coveted super-secret known only to writers, but I can share it with you. Especially since you have that I-promise-to-tell-no-one look on your face. We writers cannot write unless we have a cup, vase, or oddly-painted, ceramic cowboy boot made by our Auntie M set on our desks jammed full of an impressive array of pens and pencils, markers and highlighters.

Yes, our cup-o-writing instruments is tantamount to a full barrage of underground missiles held securely in place deep in underground bunkers right next to dismantled bunkers that have been re-purposed into living quarters for those who do not wish to see the sunrise, or set foot upon Mother Earth at ground level ever again. But I digress…

Even in this age of plastic-covered, electronic-filled boxes with lighted screens that magically draw letters from fleeting fingers onto blank pages, we desire if not need that cup of friends always at the ready. Despite the presence of devil boxes that produce stories without so much as a whiff of pine pencil shavings or the taste of chewed erasers, we still need and dream about that pacifier-of-yesteryears writing instrument. *The pencil!*

It's not often, but when there's a super moon, all is quiet, and we are alone with our straight-as-soldiers little writin' friends, we clean out our coveted cups. We only do this when, for the umpteenth time, we have reached for a pen that is too dry to make a mark on a page without gouging the paper. Maybe we will clean out our vessel after a nonchalant grab repeatedly produces the same broken pencil. After all, we writers are just too full of ourselves to stop and sharpen pencils for Heaven's sake!

In said-pencil's defense, it is not broken at the tip; it's broken inside the barrel. It is still useful! By holding it just right, one can still jot notes to remind us of fleeting thoughts we might want to expand on later. For some unexplained reason as we get, let's just say, *more mature*, those jotted notes take the place of the gray matter in our heads that we used to use to remember. Digressing again…

The "clean-out" can be described as a reunion-love-hate-funeral event. Like, discovering the Mont Blanc pen you found for just ten bucks at a yard sale is a fake. Damn!

Or the reunion with that lime-green pencil which, for some reason, has always felt just right. All smooth to the touch and its lime-green too! Who *doesn't* love lime-green?

Love surrounds you all over again when you hold in your hot, little hand that nifty double-clicker pen you accidently brought home from your friends' office.

Hate. Hmm, maybe not hate; that's such an extreme word. Let's go with intensely dislike. You so intensely dislike the trips to the dentist – no, you *hate* the trips to the dentist! Yeah, that works for me. But you are reminded of the dentist when you push down on the pen's clicker that is molded into the shape of an incisor; somehow, that pen followed you home after your last cleaning. Magically, it was redeployed from his office cup-o-pens to yours. How does that happen? HAHA

Funeral arrangements are made for all those writing utensils that just cannot be saved, no matter how many times you stick pen tips into fire to entice the ink to come out before the end becomes a melted glob.

Alas, some pencils are too short to be sharpened or haven't even a hint of an eraser left. But nobody knows what has happened to the erasers for, as we writers know, everything we write is perfect. We *never* need erasers! Moving on…

After many tears are shed for those dead or dying tools of creation, those sticks that cannot be resuscitated, one by one they are ceremoniously tossed into the round file under our desks with one last *ka-thunk*. Then, we begin a new journey to repopulate our collection.

So, covet your pens and pencils – we writers are always on the prowl to bring new friends home… Especially the lime-green ones!

44

That'll never Happen to Me

For Dave

While reading a story about a group of friends that climbed mountains all over the world and lived through an avalanche or two, I realize something – *that'll never happen to me*. I don't climb mountains. Crumb, I have a hard time climbing my little kitchen stool to get to the top shelf where I have hidden the last tin of Christmas cookies!

I used to keep score at bowling tournaments – it was really fun – and once I saw a man bowl a perfect game of 300. *That'll never happen to me*. Although I did once or twice bowl in the 200 range. It was the high end of the 100s actually, but really close to 200. Actually, the closest I will ever come to being a bowling pro is my acquaintanceship with a woman whose husband is a pro bowler. I think that is pretty cool and close enough to make a mark in the column of knowing a pro bowler.

There was a news item on my computer recently that reported some actress/singer just put her home on the market for 150 million dollars. *That'll never happen to me*. I did, however, just the other day, build a little cardboard home for a momma cat and her two new kittens. She checked out each corner and then began to purr contentedly. I don't think she would trade it for a 150-million-dollar mansion with ten bedrooms and 20 full bathrooms.

Sometimes those that'll-never-happen-to-me things in life seem to be bigger and more important than the that-happened-to-me events. But are they really?

One wonderful summer day in Eastern Nevada, a girlfriend and I took a ride up into the mountains, hiked a ways, and then had a little lunch. As we sat in a grove of shimmering leafy Aspen trees looking at the carvings of years of Basque sheep herders that had used the spot before us, we were startled by one of those herders. He came out of nowhere. He couldn't speak English and we were not fluent in Peruvian. But on the side of that mountain, we figured out that he had lost his sheep and wanted to know if we had seen them! It wasn't an avalanche event, but it was as close to climbing a mountain that I will ever come to. **Yes, that happened to me.**

One Christmas when I was a teenager, I had the notion to gather up a bunch of friends to go caroling. It was snowing as we slid up and down the streets popping off one season's greeting after another. Eventually, we found ourselves in a restaurant where some company was having a Christmas party and the employees were having a rousing good time. They invited us in and after our loud and oh-so-merry rendition of "We Wish You a Merry Christmas," they passed a hat and gave us a nice tip. **Yes, that happened to me.**

However, there are a few things we all do that we feel are unique to ourselves. Like, I pick up little rocks – pebbles really – about the size of a pea just because they are pretty and I know that one day I will pick up one that is a gold nugget. But I don't pick up big rocks or bring rocks of any size home for a rock garden/collection. My mother did that and I know a few rockers that still do which adds to their uniqueness. Okay, so that's not climbing Mt. Kilimanjaro, but it does have to do with rocks and the like.

The achievement curve is as wide or narrow as you make it. Just because you don't have a voice that would excite the judges on *The Voice*, for goodness sake, don't let that deter you from singing in the rain as loud as you want to. **Yep, that'll happen to me every once in a while.**

Not to wax too philosophically, it might take a while but I really believe that if you look long enough, work within your own settings and not those of someone else, take the hard path and make it yours, that you will, at some point in your life, finally say, "Yep! That'll happen to me."

It did for me – took some time, but now I happily write to make people smile. *Whew*. Uh, you did smile, didn't you?

45

Conformity?

For Dandy

Okay, take a deep breath as here are, hopefully, the last words to end yet another holiday season.

When I recently opened my e-mail, I found a note from a friend which needed to be pulled and tugged out from all that yuck and clutter that occasionally invades my inbox. You know, gunk that makes you wonder, how *did* Ms. Idiocy from halfway around the world get a hold of my email and *why* did she feel the need to ask *me* to financially support her so she could escape from her baboon of a husband who beats small kittens with sticks and, judging from the attached picture, wears the biggest brightest orange and purple shirts known to mankind – and on and on. How did *she* get past my spam filter? Click, delete, and move on.

My friend's note brought well wishes and a request of conformity to making New Year's resolutions. Well, maybe it leaned more toward a lack of participation in those dang resolutions. She was adamant that I conform and hold up a new resolution – know yourself to know you'll never keep a resolution.

Quite a merry-go-round we spin on during the resolution season, isn't it? I won't bother you with the do's and don'ts we make and break during this time; rather, let's take a jab at conformity.

Yes, yes, we all at one time or another conform to the world around us. To conform means to adjust yourself to act as others might. To go with social pressures. We vote and then the time-honored thing to do socially is to gripe about the winners. Sometimes we eat too much. Then, as we sit uncomfortably on our Barcaloungers, it seems to have become socially acceptable to moan about the uncomfortableness of the meal gurgling in our tummies. We buy a new anything then, on the chance we see an advertisement about our new purchase, we gripe about the price we paid because another store a mere 50 miles away had the same something on sale for less.

But conforming can also have positive consequences within the social pressure cooker.

We go to church and pray with like-minded parishioners and feel warm and fuzzy. We hold a new baby and say what a wonderful smell a clean baby has and take a deep breath. We look at a sunset that radiates a glow of crimson, orange, and amber and in awe, we conformists admit we want it to last forever. I sense you are thinking about a recent baby or a sunset in the recesses of your mind. Well, come back to Earth.

In these times, conforming, or not, to making and keeping resolutions has become a resolution in itself. I will not tell my over-indulged self that I will do better this year. I will not try to answer every text I get. There seems to always be more things not to do than to do when climbing the resolution ladder. So, as aghast as it may seem, there are things I will do because I have done them before and they work for me.

I will still gripe about too much snow on my deck, but I will still enjoy shoveling it even though it drove my other half crazy that I venture outside when it was below freezing. I will always buy too many fresh vegetables at one time and then chide myself as I throw out a smooched and somewhat hairy tomato that was found hiding in the back of the veggie drawer next to the stalks of limp celery that are too far gone for even soup. I will laugh aloud, cry because the cutest kitten in the litter didn't make it, and re-tell the story of what happened during a family photo opportunity that resulted in a nutty picture. In short – oh, like I can brief about anything – I will continue to happily be me, warts and all.

But in light of a new dawn, I wish to thank you, my ITY-Inputters, and those who read these fun remembrances and pull your own memories out of your own cobwebs to enjoy.

Now *that* is a resolution I can easily and joyfully keep each week.

Hey! Happy New Year!

46

Apples and Oranges
For Rich

Don't you agree that it is human nature to compare? My hair, her hair. Their truck, our truck. Your kids, the neighbor's kids. Oh, I have always said that if I had kids, they would have been the best kids – ever. Like your kids! But since the world did not grace me with a brood of my own, I have come to compare all kids by the "your kids, my neighbor's kids" thought process.

Comparing makes for good contests in life. It all starts with that age-old school yard proclamation, "Oh yeah? Well, *my* dad can beat up *your* dad." I have yet to see two dads who have been touted as being the best pugilist, go a round or two just for the sake of their kid's honor. Thankfully. But as far as comparing goes, no matter how good, better, or best you think your anything is, there is someone with a bigger, better, or best-est everything just waiting in the wings to dangle their better-equipped do-hickey in front of you.

So, here is what you do to even out the playing field of life. Apple and orange them.

Yes, apple and orange them.

They say their dog is a better hunter than your fine beast named Duffy. So, you say Ole Duffy can eat a ground squirrel in one gulp. Ah, now without even breaking a sweat, you have not only said what kind of hunter your dog is, but that he is a hunter and can get a ground squirrel, a feat that does not lose any luster to your friend's proclamation of his dog's hunting ability. After all, most of us know that catching an in-the-ground-hiding-ground squirrel is quite a coo. Not only that, but your dog could out-eat this other hunting dog! You see, even though both dogs are held in the highest regard by both owners, their traits are apples and oranges.

Here is another comparison. A friend scoots up in a brand-new truck, a *really* nice truck adorned in chrome and shine. He gets out, stepping down off the automatic running boards. It has, as my dad would say, "hot and cold running everything." Now, you should know that I am very excited when someone buys a new vehicle. It is a big deal, especially now that a new car or truck will probably cost as much as my new house did back in the eighties. Uh, the 1980s. Smarty pants!

Any way, you want to be happy about this new vehicle purchase, but that comparison, human-nature-of-life contest is up and running at full throttle. So, to feed that green-eyed monster, you walk all the way around his new truck, maybe give out a low whistle. Perhaps you wag your hand a little for emphasis and even sit in the driver's seat while you lazily run your fingers across the dash. Push a button, turn a knob. Remark about that new-car smell, take in a deep breath, and smile.

Then, with a kind of sideway glance, you say, "Wow, this is the bomb. I remember when I bought my new truck a few years ago. Man, it was the best day ever." Then you pause for effect as your friend puffs up just a little. Then you add, "Right up until the day I paid the thing off last month." Or something along those lines. And you can actually hear a zinger-zing overhead.

This is a real apples and oranges moment. You have given kudos to the new truck owner. Even let them feel a nice pat on the back about their purchase, but then you just have to add the fact that you have also had a new truck – apples. But the best thing about your truck is that your baby is paid off – oranges! It will hang in the air that his paid-off day will be sometime far, far, *far* in the future. Maybe even five or six years down the road.

Now, I do not say this to be facetious or to promote ill will toward another person's moment of happiness; I just know that comparing and that one-upmanship mode is and always will be alive and well in all of us.

But if it wasn't like that? What if we truly were just happy that our friend had a dog that was a great hunter without having to one-up that poor dog with the accomplishments of Duffy? What if we didn't go into our houses at night and grumble to ourselves or our spouse that ole so-and-so down the street has a bigger, better, shinier do-hickey than we have ourselves?

Yeah, I don't think that will ever happen either. But I'm working on it. Sure makes you wonder though, doesn't it? Just when you think you have a handle on all the oranges and apples in your basket?

Of course, that's when your friend with the shiny, dolled-up truck looks at you and tells you with a grim face that his rich uncle with whom he was very close recently passed away, but happily left your friend a bundle so he paid cash for his new baby! *Zing!*

Yep. Human is as human does.

47

A Glass of Milk
For Carol

I can't decide whether I consider the first cool refreshing gulp or the last satisfying slurp of a glass of ice-cold milk is the best. Of course, all the swallows in between those two smile-making times are just as wonderful. The same could be said of a big gulp of soda or an ice-cold beer. But milk has a slot of its very own. Oh, and with milk, you don't get a mouth full of foam as you gulp while trying to swallow too much too fast. Hey, you could drown with soda or beer. With milk? You just smack your lips and proclaim, "Aaaahhh!"

There is an art to pouring a glass of milk when you really want, no, *crave* that cool white liquid. Of course, you could just go to the cupboard, pull out any ole glass, pour, and suck the milk down. Some will even skip the glass all together and in a rush to get that hit of milk, drink right out of the milk jug. Putting the plastic jug to your mouth and sucking the liquid out until the plastic collapses and gives way to the vacuum created when the milk travels down to your satisfied tummy. To the horror of it all, I admit I have done this. But to my credit, I have not done it since I grew up and learned about all the little germs in everyone's mouth. *Yuck.* Please don't drink from the carton unless you live alone, especially if you ever expect to have company either planned or by surprise over for milk and cookies. Okay, let's slosh along.

Before I give up my secret to creating the perfect glass of milk, here is a situation you might find yourself in – or not.

I grew up in a house of three kids and not tons of money. We were comfortable but not affluent. So, over the years there were things that were done to save a shekel here and a penny there, like cardboard in your shoes when a hole was there. It wasn't that a lack of money has been announced. In fact, I didn't realize until I was older that some money-saving shortcuts were being done. Well, one of those things that was the norm in our home was to pour milk into a glass and stop a little over halfway. At first, you might think that it was done because the kids were small and couldn't handle a full glass. But in retrospect it was to save money.

It wasn't until I had been into marriage for some time when my other half looked at me one evening and declared that I poured milk like my mom. He wanted me to know he was grown up and could have a full glass of milk! Live and learn, right? So now, I pour right up to the top – and sometimes, when I wanted to get his goat, I poured right up to the tippy top! Ah, karma.

Onto the most satisfying way to have a glass of milk, a realization, I can assure, was discovered on accident. Two things happened. When newly married, we would travel a couple hundred miles to buy groceries for a month at a time, something I still do in some regard. In doing so, we would buy milk in the waxy half-gallon paper cartons by the cases and bring them home and freeze them.

I occasionally forgot, by accident or just laziness, to take milk out to thaw before needing it. This would sometimes result in ice crystals in the poured milk. Can't you just taste the coolness? Oh yes. Other than chugging your first frozen margarita after a long Friday, the ice crystals in half-frozen milk give the *best* brain freeze.

Second, while making pudding – the kind you had to cook on the stove – I would use my metal measuring cups to measure the required milk into the pan. On a whim one day, I measured another cupful and gulped it down. It was *so* cold and refreshing out of that icy measuring cup.

So, what can you do with the knowledge of icy milk and the coolness the metal cups bring to the table when pouring milk? Well now, when the cow inside me moos with one of those cannot-dismiss urges for a cold gulp of milk, this is what I do. I take one of these wonderful enameled blue-and-white-speckled tin cups we bought just for this purpose and run our 36-degree-right-out-of-the-faucet-cold-clear-clean well water on it to chill the cup. Next, I fill that chilly cup – to the top – with milk right out of the fridge and (can you taste it?) with the gusto of a desert rat who just came upon an oasis, the perfect cup of cold wonderful milk is poured down my pie hole!

Why don't I just put that tin cup in the freezer and get it really cold? One – I just don't have the patience for that; two – the few times I have tried that, the milk literally freezes to the cup and my lips! Doesn't take a truckload of turnips to fall on this chickadee for me to learn a life lesson!

So, to recap.

> Tin cup
> Running cold water
> Milk
> Lips
> Pie hole.
> Smile as big as all outdoors!

My work here is done.

48

A Hairy World
For Carolyn

We have two house cats that shed – constantly – quietly – in clumps and singularly. Normally, that would be 'nuff said. But as per my usual, there is always so much more to say.

Trying to stay on top of shedding animals and humans is a never-ending circle of hair today, hair tomorrow. It doesn't seem to matter how much sweeping up with a broom or sucking up with a vacuum I do; there is always something floating around just looking for an eye to land in or a TV screen to stick to.

Yes, I admit, I have also found a wayward piece of myself – *a hair* – in the spaghetti. That wasn't as bad as the time my other half found a fly in the spaghetti. Huh! Maybe I should quit making spaghetti. Hmm, yes, that's the excuse I'm going with; it's the spaghetti's fault! HAHA But finding little bits of ourselves in our home cooking is not what brings me here today.

No, it's about finding someone else's hair, skin cells, or fingernails hanging out in the soup or other epicurean delight. That was the topic of discussion recently. I just shuddered – you too? Yep, there is nothing as appetizing as digging into or licking up a much-anticipated ice cream delight handed to you out a drive-thru window and finding an extra-long, or even kinky, added attraction to your dessert. Yummy. *Not!* Or maybe grabbing a potato chip out of a freshly opened bag and finding a second chip fastened to it with a string of hair... Ugh. But again, I'm not quite there...

Someone needs to explain to me why there seems to be one person more than anyone else in the family that is usually the recipient of these added bonuses. Now, I don't want to tempt the fates here, but in our house that recipient is not usually me. You might think that is a blessing, but in reality, it is easier for me to find the bonus in the meal. I will just quietly remove the added attraction and then quit the meal. I prefer to not cause a big hullabaloo.

But – yes, a hairy "but," yuck – there are those who find the need to make a display of the find. Make a big production of finding something other than mushrooms hiding under a layer of cheese on their piece of hot chewy pizza. They pull whatever it is and lay it on a fresh napkin like it is royalty. They examine it to see if it has come from a member of the immediate family or if it is something that was lost from some unknown unseen contributor in a factory somewhere far, far away. Or if it is now or ever was alive! *Double yuck!* Then, with a proper look of disgust on their face, they call attention to the object and make those gagging sounds, pushing their plate across the table like it is on fire. They grab for water with the theatrics of a pubescent middle schooler. And on and on…

To go further on this oh-so-mouthwatering subject but along a different road, what do you do when you get a hair in your eye? This is really annoying especially if you have a cat or dog that has really fine hair in residence. Again, this happens to the hair magnet in our family more often anyone else.

In the past, it wasn't a problem to help get the unwanted intruder out of the eye. We would start by making what we call a ninny kind of twist to one corner of a tissue to be used as a scoop to gather and remove the unwanted intruder. That worked for years. But I have recently noticed, and my other half has too, that the hairs that come in contact with the eyes in our house are getting smaller and smaller like Alice and the whole rabbit-hole catastrophe. I have to set my glasses just so to be able to access the extra thick part – the bifocal part – so I can see the eye I am digging around in. That means I have to get really close to the victim and that is getting to be more and more uncomfortable as it involves bending in weird ways. Now it seems easier to just have a bottle of eye drops or artificial tears on hand to wash the eye out.

More interesting is when you have to find something in your own eye and you wear glasses. That can become a merry hunt in itself.

Let me end here by going completely off track – of course, whoever heard of me going off track? I want to talk about hair and the lack of it and/or too much of it… I am more than happy that in recent years so much research and development has gone into finding new ways to grow hair. Baldness is a billion-dollar business and there is a growing concern – get it? Baldness/growing concern? Anyway, hair can now be grown in ways that had never before been grown. *Hurray!* But as a woman who has gone through "the change" and has found that strangely there is now hair growing in places that a woman usually doesn't have hair… Well, I think it is about time that some expanded R&D money be spent on getting rid of hair as fervently as things have been done for those who want to grow hair!

Actually, there is a long way to go on this short-sided subject, so I think it will be best if I cut it off here, blow dry on to something else, and leave this to get a good shellacking for another day.

I can, however, give ninny-making instructions if the need arises.

49

An Impatient patient
For Randy

If you have never been lucky enough to encounter an impatient patient in a waiting room, take heart. Eventually you will be privy to a scene you will tell your friends about over and over because you still, even after watching it unfold right in front of you, don't believe what you saw. This goes beyond the upset small-fry being fussy. This territory covers the patient who needs to be somewhere else and that somewhere else is much more important than being a *patient* patient waiting in the waiting room.

Let's talk about this impatient patient. First, an appointment had to be made at some point in time. I feel very lucky to live where I live. We have a nice clinic and great providers who are available usually the same day we call. Where else is that need met without involving an ER at the nearest hospital? A very advantageous advantage to living in our small community. But it doesn't matter if you get in the same day or if you have to wait any amount of time, if an appointment is made, you have to know that a block of your time needs to be carved out of your day to go, meet, keep, and have your appointment. How hard is that to do? I mean, come on. *You* made the appointment!

Yes, I know. Sometimes things happen and new appointments mess with existing ones. Trust me; I have had it happen. But an important thing I learned along the way is this: "Poor planning on your part does not make an emergency on my part." Or vice versa. In other words, if you find the need to stand at a counter and rag on a poor receptionist because your hair dresser needed to change your appointment because she needs to go to see her palm reader a few hours earlier because her palm reader didn't know that her babysitter needed to leave earlier than expected because her mother needed a ride to the airport to pick up her sister who decided to fly in a day early because the rates went down and she saved 5 bucks – *frantic breathing* – then that's your problem.

Keeping with the medical side of impatience, I once talked to a pharmacist who had dealt with a few impatient patients. One particular couple stood out in her memory. Oh, when impatience has back-up in the form of a *second* impatient person, you know you're in for double trouble! The deal was that they needed medicine, whatever it was, and they needed it right now! You and I know that no matter what kind of medicine you take, be it for acne or zinc toxicity, it will not be spontaneously ready for you upon your arrival – unless you have one of those automated pharmacy text-message notifications. Additionally, once ingested, medicine takes time to take effect. With those in mind, wouldn't a bit of decorum be appreciated?

The time it took for the impatient patient to demand, the pharmacist to kindly explain that they weren't the only ones in need of medication, and the impatient patient to fume could have been spent on moving the process along. But the impatient patient could not understand this. Instead, the impatient patient fussed and raged. Oh, and by the way, this particular impatient patient had just spent more than a few hours in an ER – waiting. Wonder what that was like for the ER staff?

It probably sounds nuts, but I rather enjoy short one-act plays put on by impatient patients, like the one where the woman stood at the sliding glass window in a doctor's office going on and on about her Patient Protection and Affordable Care Act insurance, aka, Obama Care, how she was covered, how it was paid for by Obama, how she should be first in line because of it, how she could just snap her fingers and Obama would walk in checkbook in hand, how – well, you get the jest of it. Yes, I meant to say "jest!" The receptionist was cool and collected. Apparently, this was not her first rodeo ride. Quite jesting, a.k.a. entertaining.

Now, I'm not saying there isn't a time and place to not be patient. If you find yourself sitting next to someone who is turning blue, for goodness sake, stand up and be the most impatient person in the room by screeching, "Hey, this guy is turning *blue*!"

I have heard stories of patients who wait weeks or even months for appointments. I, thankfully, have not had that happen – yet. But if I did and I even remembered after months of waiting why I had appointment, I would keep it, I would be on time, and I would be ready to wait – just sitting back to enjoy the free show in the waiting room.

Of course, you never do get to see the end of the show as your name is usually called just before the climax and you're forced to leave the theater – *ahem* – waiting room.

Happens all the time.

50

Advice-full Advisors
For Reynard

Will there ever be an age when we get to, or can, stop taking advice? Not the loving advice that is meant to make our lives easier, smoother, or safer. No. I want to address advice like how to clean a toilet. Okay, here's the story. You're on the edge of your seat, aren't you? Hope it isn't the toilet seat!

I have been cleaning toilets for as long as I can remember. Not to brag about it but, I've had my head down in more than a few toilets in my womanhood. I have tried a bathtub load of cleaners which all seem to clean about the same. Some bubble up and cause a stink. Some just cling and wait to be coaxed to clean. Some turn the water a delightful shade of blue that is supposed to make you think you need to hop into the happy hull of a boat and skim across the top of the water in the bowl. I have no idea who would want that, but there it is, refreshingly blue and, in someone's eyes, inviting. Pretty poopy if you ask me.

Then I read an article published by a guy who purports to be a master plumber who says that all the hundreds of dollars I have spent on cleaners across the years was a waste of money. Really? So naturally, I read faster to find out just what the secret was to keeping the unmentionable sight from getting more unmentionable.

The toilet bowl brush. Yep, that's apparently all it takes as per this advice-full advisor. Let's just take a closer look at this little tidbit of knowledge. So, you go into the bathroom armed with a brush and good intentions. I should say here that he advised doing this every day. Right off I can tell you that I don't know anyone who has time to scratch toilet cleaning into their *daily* schedule. Maybe we can all train ourselves and the others in our families that after they are done on the throne, they are to turn around and brush the bowl. Yeah, I'm pretty sure that might last, like, two days at the most! I can just imagine what a six-year-old with a bowl brush and an unflushed toilet could create. Sloshing on…

Why, you may be asking, does this recommendation come from the mouth of a master plumber? I would hazard a guess that he got burnt at some time buying some toilet cleaner company stock that tanked – punk intended! His advice is that the chemicals just don't do as good a job as the brush. He goes on to say that the cleaners may, in fact, cause a clog! Oh, come on! Moreover, he claims drain cleaners are not your friend either. A good ole plunger is your best bet – unless you have a drain snake. But the use of a snake may cause damage to your pipes so if the plunger fails, call a plumber. Man, oh man! Just where has this silver-tongued devil been all my life?

I finally decided my new plumbing friend was full of it. Using just a brush wouldn't get near enough of the stuff out of his bowl full of advice!

In reality, there is wonderful advice out there to give and get, like when being served food in a Mexican restaurant, don't touch that hot plate they've just warned you is hot. But, of course, we all give the plate a little push, don't we?

Or how you should lace up that boot before you go out to shovel the snow or you might fall down and break your crown. That one is, of course, also from personal experience. I'm thinking my new boots should have zippers.

How in the world do you know which advice to take to heart and which to take with a grain of salt? I would say common sense, but there seems to be less and less of that around. Maybe experience really is the grand teacher.

But what if you are just coming online to the housework world? How could you know that a bowl brush just isn't going to "cut it?" The same way you learned that you don't go outside when it is thundering and there is lightning dancing the La Bamba around your house. The same way you learned that everyone isn't right when they tell you to jump off the roof into the pool. The same way you learned not to eat yellow snow. *Yikers!*

Take advice from trusted people around you. Chances are that they learned whatever they are advising you about in a way that you don't really want to know.

On the other hand, hilarious and/or self-preservation experiences you will have along your life path will give you the authority to become an Advice-full Advisor.

51

A Pro-crastinator
For Dan G

A while ago – well, more than a while ago… okay, years ago – I heard a story that still makes me laugh. Seems there was this doctor who thought he was bigger than life. He had a tendency to let his head get a tad bit too big. You know the type! It doesn't have to be a doctor; it could really be anyone who thinks they are "all that." I venture to say we probably all know someone like that.

Warning: If you say you don't know anyone who fits that description, there is a distinct possibility you are that type of person.

Well, this doctor was having trouble with a phone in his office – this was pre-cell phones. The line to his private phone in his inner sanctum office had a bit of a scratchy sound to it. Not a big deal. However, to this doctor, it was in need of immediate attention, but only after hours. Couldn't have a repairman in his office during business hours for goodness sake. So, he procrastinated in calling the phone company until evening. Well, he didn't actually call the company. He knew the local phone guy and called him at home one evening and requested, well, in his overly important voice, *told* the phone guy to drop everything and get to his office to fix that oh-so-important phone line. After all, he was a doctor and needed that phone fixed!

The phone guy, a surly but quick-witted man who had a few scotch and sodas under his belt on this particular evening while at home relaxing, listened to the rants of the doctor and then as pretty as you please, replied, "Give it two aspirins and call me in the morning," and hung up. Priceless.

Now, I tell you that story for two reasons. Firstly, I think it is funny. Come on, who wouldn't want to be in the position to tell the doctor to take two aspirins and call back in the morning? More to the point, it shows that procrastination runs in us all and I think it is human nature to expect our procrastination to be fixed by someone else. In my world, my procrastination is my own darn problem. I sometimes – not all the time, mind you – can be a **pro-crastinator**.

Oh, you have to get up pretty early in the morning to let things slide as well as I can. I'm not talking just leaving the dinner dishes until morning, which I have done only to regret that life decision the following dawn as I trottle into the kitchen. Yes trottle…

Trottle (v.): to scuff one's feet along the floor until coffee has been ingested and caffeine has been introduced to the system.

I don't like to trottle into the kitchen in the morning only to get smacked in the face with the smell of last night's meatloaf complete with congealed grease and hardened green beans on smeared dishes. *Yuck!*

No, the **pro** part of my pro-crastination goes deeper than that. Like bill paying. I don't really mind paying bills. I don't like it but, I create bills, I need to pay bills. I buy, therefore, I am woman, right? Anyway. I am not sure exactly when it happened, but I have begun to leave this task until the eleventh hour. I used to get a bill and pay it the same day. *Zip, bam, boom* – done. But recently, I have found I leave piles of mail on the breakfast bar counter until I have no room to place my evening snack of cookies and milk. I have become a **pro-crastinator** – cue the heavy-handed music.

A side note to the gal I talked to at the power company. I really did mail the check in time! I may be slow, but not late. That is not in my DNA!

There are a multitude of things in life to procrastinate over. I still haven't washed my windows this year. But – yes, a procrastinating "but" – fall is on the horizon. Maybe I'll let the windows go without washing until next spring. I mean, you've seen one snow storm and snow drifts grow upon the land, you've seen them all, right?

Sometimes I mow the lawn but don't do the trimming. Ah, it'll wait until next week.

I'm sitting here looking at the dust that has accumulated on my printer, a dark-gray sleek model that sits at eye level. I'll get to it. Tomorrow. Hey it still prints, dust covering and all.

The big difference between me being a **pro-crastinator** and me being a lazy butt? I *notice* that I am procrastinating and eventually I do the things I've been putting off. Hey, if I didn't, eventually I wouldn't even be able to see out the windows. And I have a great view out my window. Okay, excuse me, I'm going to get the Windex out, uh… in a few minutes.

Once a **pro-crastinator**, always a pro. Living in Nevada where in some places prostitution is legal, I guess I shouldn't throw the word "pro" around so easily!

52

A Mystery-Flavored Day
For Kendra

I was at the bank the other day waiting to hear yet again that there is never enough money in my account, when I picked out one of the free suckers waving at me from the little bucket on the counter next to the window where I stood. I should have known from the name of the suckers – Dum Dums – that my day was destined to be yet another test. AARRGGHH.

First off, I usually prefer berry-flavored suckers. Not a weird berry, just a regular berry – straw, ras, or blue. So, I picked the little sucker by the color of the wrapper (red) since I didn't have my glasses on and there was no way I could read the tiny writing on the wrapper. I assumed – which I know I should never do – it would be something like strawberry. I stuffed the sucker in my bank bag for later. I mean, I didn't want to seem like I was there just for the suckers. I do have *some* etiquette.

I finished my business with the teller and the next few things that happened I blame totally on that sucker! I dropped my bank bag as I left the window and the roll of fifty-cent pieces I had just received split open. A few of the shiny coins escaped, rolling across the smooth linoleum floor in every direction. *Swell.*

Now, that isn't too much of a thing, except have you noticed as you get older, the ground gets further and further away? So, having to contort, like, six times in a row to pick up flat half-dollars from the unforgiving tiled floor was challenging to say the least. The down wasn't so bad; it was the coming back up that was a real bugger! My change in hand, red-faced, I left the bank, sucker still tucked away in the bag – waiting.

Oh, did you come away from that last little tale wondering why anyone would get a roll of 50-cent pieces? Well, it's just a thing I do sometimes. I like to leave them as tips. I used to get them as tips when I was a waitress in a small casino I worked at and I kept them longer than any other coins I can remember. I liked having them on hand when all the other money was gone. They saved me more than once when I needed extra cash. I know, just another Trina quirk. I'm betting that most people have some quirk they keep in their bag of life... Don't you? If not, feel free to use my 50-cent piece quirk!

After my bank fiasco, purchasing weed spray was next on my list. At the garden store, I picked up a jug whose lid was askew which I attempted to straighten. Should have heard that little voice yelling, "Sucker!" I screwed it on too tight and cracked the jug, sending noxious weed spray gurgling down aisle nine...

Next on my list was hair color. I wasn't going to a salon, only purchasing some in case someday I might want to give it a try. *Wink, wink.* So, I'm looking at the hundreds of packages when I picked one up... and dropped it. It wasn't my fault. It was a slick container, all shiny and smooth and filled with blue hair dye. Yep, the voice in my head hollered, "Sucker!" A wet and smelly liquid slithered down aisle four.

Next the grocery store, but given my recent history of the day, was it really needed? Needed pickles; passed the pickle jars. Needed mayonnaise; passed the mayonnaise jars. Needed a jar of spaghetti sauce; *definitely* passed the jars of spaghetti sauce! For the next few meals anyway, we would be eating things that came from a box. A nice, sturdy box!

This shopping excursion took place out of town so I had a couple hours to drive to get home. Time to re-group, gather myself, and put the day behind me. During the drive, I spotted that bank bag on the seat next to me and thought about that sucker. Laughing at all the mishaps and thumbing my nose at that fate-thingy, I grabbed the bag, dug out the sucker, unwrapped it, stuck it in my pie hole, and began to slobber at it.

I couldn't figure out the berry flavor – straw, ras, or blue. Well, it wasn't blueberry as it was this kinda pinkish color. After a few licks and swallows, I had no idea what I was consuming so I un-wadded the wrapper. I now had my glasses on as I was driving.

The wrapper announced that what I held was a "mystery flavor."

My day did not need another surprise, so I pitched the sucker, turned up the radio, and drove the rest of the way home singing as loud as I could to scatter any lingering bad karma toadies riding along with me. Very therapeutic.

53

The Best Afterschool Home
For Arlene

It's getting to be that time of year. Cooler evenings –
and mornings. Fall is falling. Guys wearing blaze-orange over
camo are getting ready for hunting season. New empty-
nesters are buying up boxes and boxes of Kleenex, readying
themselves for the sad quietness that will surround them as
their last birdie leaves the nest while crying with jubilation of
such well-deserved *freedom*! Like yellow and black caterpillars
that have been lazily waiting for fall, here come the yellow
school buses out of their hibernation hidey-holes. If back-to-
school activity hasn't hit your neighborhood yet, it will shortly
and many a parent will dance the happy dance of "school's
back in session."

I talked to a man the other day who was getting ready
to go to his 55th class reunion. Yes, 55 years. We agreed that
one never truly gets all the way out of high school. I wonder
if I will make it to my 55th reunion. I have a long, long way
to go. Okay, maybe just a long way to go. HAHA

I don't know as many kids here as I probably should,
but that is because I don't travel in the school circle in our
area. I hear stuff about the school. I know people on the
school board. I know where the schools are. I pay my taxes
and part of those go toward the running of the schools. But
that's about the extent of me and our local schools. That
doesn't pique my interest. I'm more interested in what the
tykes do *after* school.

Now and then a conversation will take you back. The
smell of burnt coffee takes you to a campfire where the

coffee boiled over and you then find yourself remembering that whole trip. The sight of someone getting a haircut puts you in that chair the day you got that *way-too-curly* perm and you cried all the way to the store to get an off-the-shelf perm to straighten those oh-so-lovely locks you overpaid for – and even left a nice tip. Dang me, I have to get over that experience one day! Well, this past week, I was reminded of the "afterschool house" on our block when I was a kid.

Seems like every neighborhood has that one especially-great home that most of the kids hang out at after school. The mom, or in today's world, maybe the dad is there when the kids who live there and all their friends hit the door afterschool. Snacks are there. The yard is clean. The home is inviting.

There was a home like that on the block where I lived when I was a kid. A conversation I had with a block mom of today reminded me of the block mom we had – Mrs. Playford. Amazing that her name had play in it, huh? She was always ready for a house full of kids.

Oh, there were other homes to go to after school. There was the family where the mother made us take off our shoes before we came in. Boo. We had to wash our hands. Boo again. The snacks were dry fruit. We didn't go there much.

There was the girl whose father worked at an ice cream distributor center. They always had ice cream sandwiches in their freezer. Hurray! But the kids were real mean, so a lot of us didn't go there much either. Ice cream or not, we did have our standards. Mean is always ugly. Was then and still is today.

When I was a kid, my house occasionally got the herd of after-schoolers. The grass in our yard sometimes took a real beating from bikes and cardboard sleds. You know, doing all those fun things kids do.

The whole afterschool home came up when I was talking to a young mom the other day. Turns out her home was an afterschool home for her kids and their friends. Kids don't care that there are dishes in the sink. Kids are not impressed if your carpet isn't vacuumed. Kids just want popsicles and someone to notice them. Just to be there, to be available to them.

This block mom of today was cute. She said the kids run up to her as she gets home from her job that lets her be home shortly after the kids get there. They are all over her. She tried to bemoan to me that she couldn't even get in the house to change out of her work clothes. But in her eye, there was a little twinkle that said she wouldn't have had it any other way.

Of course, as kids grow up, there are loads of afterschool activities. But when you have a pile of, say, 8 to12-year-olds? If you can, make your home the afterschool go-to home. You will be able to put those memories on your pillow every night and you will be giving the kids some "Mrs. Playford" memories that will last forever too. Memories that will create grown-ups who will want to create and have the after-school home on their block when they have kids – and then their kids will do it and their kids' kids… What would be better than that?

Drive safe – school is always in session somewhere.

54

A Battery of Questions

For Pete

I've had to jump a battery to get a car going. Or a tractor, or a four-wheeler, or a lawn mower... It was drilled into my pea brain that "black on-black off" is the correct hook 'em and unhook 'em sequence. It's a right of car-ownership passage to have jumped a battery at least once. Like the first time you run out of gas because you didn't listen to the subtle *ding-ding-ding* of the fuel gauge reminding you to stop for push water.

With "hook up" lessons, you also get schooled on battery chargers, trickle chargers, battery load testing, and – my favorite – battery cables. Cables are defined as either black or red. A fun way to remember the rules of jumping a car is as follows:

Black goes on black and red goes on red. If you get those screwed up you get zapped, sending sparks everywhere and scaring the you-know-what out of you!

You'll learn about 6 and 12-volt batteries. The easiest way to tell 6V from 12V – a 6V has three of those little caps on the top where the acid would be added while the 12V has 6 caps.

Really?

Why wouldn't the 6V have 6 caps and the 12V have 12 caps? If I were queen of the world, that's how it would be, but batteries will not change just because I think they should. Just remember, three means six and six means twelve. Good luck with that.

Why am I speaking in battery circles? Well, here's the electrifying story. I'm assuming you know that when and if a car doesn't cough to life upon the turn of a key, your battery needs resuscitation a.k.a. a jumpstart or a charge; or maybe it just needs to be fully replaced.

I know one should never assume – I'm sticking my neck out here – but nobody likes the *rur-rur-rur* of a dead or dying battery. And worse is having to jump the car, boat, airplane, etc. If after an unsuccessful jump, your vehicular transport remains dead, then replacing the battery is the next expensive option. Well, that's where things nowadays may just get a little strange and complicated. It did for a couple I know who hopefully will not mind if I tell this story.

It was friends. No, no. *Really!* Not *everything* happens to me, you know.

So, this friend and her other half took all of the car owner steps of dead-battery fixes after she went out to start the car and all she got was the aforementioned *rur-rur-rur* and no *varoom*. You know the dead battery fixes of spitting into the wind, turning clockwise three times and bowing at the waist to the East. None of those worked. After all the ill-fated fate avenues of resuscitation had been exhausted, it was decided that a jump or replacement of the dead black box battery was the final solution. Luckily the car was in their yard so it should be a snap to accomplish.

But luck has two sides, you know.

The wife had known enough to open the hood and hook up the charger to the points under the hood that were very visibly marked to necessitate a charge. "Put positive here" and "put negative here" were the bright signs she saw under the hood. All very up front. But she noticed the cables were not attached to the battery like usual – *Maybe it had something to do with the electronics of this newer vehicle*, she thought. She tried the jump avenue to no avail. So new battery was the final solution.

After some discussion and a call to the local parts' store to see if a battery was in stock – it was – she purchased a battery and was promised that if she brought down the dead one as soon as it was disconnected, she would be given a core charge refund. Oh? The core charge? There is a whole other discussion to have about the automotive parts world. HAHA

Anyway, back to the story at hand. So, the new battery was brought home and set next to the sad-faced, juiceless car. Then the fun really began.

With the hood open, wrenches in hand to disconnect the battery, well, that's when things got weird. They couldn't find the battery. Not on the left or right side of the engine. Not in the front or toward the back. They poked, bent, looked, and even got down and peered underneath. Nope, no battery was to found. After some calm – yes, *calm* – discussion, a call was hesitantly placed to the dealer where the car had been purchased. It took three mechanics and several just-a-minute pauses before a revelation was achieved.

The battery? Nope, not under the hood. It was *hidden* in the *floor* under the carpet *behind* the passenger seat!

Seriously? Who would've looked there?

Now, I know late Model T cars from the early 1900s had batteries in a box behind the seat and Mercedes have batteries in the trunk. But come on, after years of the battery being under the hood? Who took it upon themselves to change this?

I was going to be facetious and make mention of who I thought had come up with this. But I better just let it go and learn from my friends who now laugh as they play, "Battery, battery, where's the battery?"

55

55 Was a Very Fine Year

Continuing My Ever-Evolving Education
For You!

I was once told to learn one new thing every day. Good advice – but harder than chewing rock candy to keep up with. Try it, if even for a week. A new word, a new way to curl your hair, mayo or miracle whip on your tuna sandwich (mayo, of course!).

Any one thing,
every day,
for one entire 7-day week.

Oh, it's possible, but it is demanding and harder than you think. Who knew you could cram new stuff into your brain no matter your age?

Just as hard as learning is teaching, explaining, telling, expressing, or otherwise delivering your knowledge to the world. Harder still is not delivering your knowledge to the world – in other words, keeping your pie hole shut and your opinions to yourself (a lesson I hope I have learned, but that does not make it any easier to adhere by). And that is where I found myself recently, wanting to speak up, tell my opinion, speak my mind, and let my pie hole go whole-hog, as it were. But I did not go forth and I am still undecided if quiet was the right path to take.

I had to heed yet another piece of advice I got when I was but a youngster and my mouth ruled my mind, instead of my mind ruling my mouth. If you can't say something nice, don't say anything at all. That is what kept me silent and my inside thoughts inside my head. But what would have happened had I spoken up? What happens when you speak your mind?

Well, this is what happens. You get all the stares in the room, burning into you like your hair is on fire. You hear gasps and the air is sucked out of the room and passes over your head so fast that if you had a hat on, it would have ended up in the next county. Your comments become fodder for the grapevine and beyond. Your stance on the subject you felt compelled to speak on is now in the record books for all eternity. Knowing all that, knowing that when you speak up, especially when you are on the small side of the yard divided by a white picket fence, is it worth it? You bet your sweet Bippy it is!

Maybe spontaneous combustion is a result of holding in or holding back things you really want to say to someone. Like telling a good friend that moving across the country is not the best thing for them. Or saying to someone you care deeply about that they are making a huge life mistake by just running from one thing to another without growing where they are planted.

Could I explode, actually explode, if I keep the aforementioned pie hole shut and not mention that no matter how badly you want to go home again, you can't? It is never the same once you have been out in the world. And for you to expect it to be the same is a pipe dream and not fair to you or the family you are moving back to be by.

Nope, I can't say everything I want to say because I am of the old school that keeps their noses on their own side of the fence. Harder to get it chopped off that way, you see. It's that part of me that still believes it is best to say something nice or say nothing. That part of me keeps me quiet and that makes me seem standoffish or even uncaring. Better standoffish than have a bitter taste left in the mouth, I say.

I continue to educate myself all the time as to which path to take. The easy path is not usually the best path which makes the best path usually turn out to not be the easy path. So, we all bump along, fall occasionally, be picked up, and help others up too. But not saying what is on your mind is a daily decision we make. What makes it fun is that we actually do get to make that decision. Flip a coin, pull the short straw, or draw a decision out of a hat. No matter how you decide when making a decision – to run your mouth or put a stopper in that hole under your nose – it's ultimately your responsibility. Then you will sleep at night. Promise.

Oh, and along these same lines, if I don't add this, then all the times I heard it over and over from my parents as I was growing up will have been for naught...

"Trina! Children are to be *seen* and not *heard*."

I hear that every time, every stinking time I open my mouth to put my two cents into a conversation. Or to give advice. Or, and this one is a big one, before I *ask* for advice! Yes, sometimes it is best to keep the pie hole just jam-packed full of pie, uh, instead of words.

Of course, if I always keep my pie hole shut, how in the world could I ever be so happy and feel so rewarded by writing down nearly everything my brain thinks?

If I keep my mouth shut, then how would I share those fascinating, fun, frivolous, and forthright tales of human nature with as many people as possible – like you?

Some Final Fun Stuff

It's not often you get the chance to tell an author just what you think. I openly invite you to become one of the few, the funny, the fabulous ITY-Inputters. Write to me like those who sent me the following notes… Yes! I do answer each one.

You take the time to say "Hi!" and so will I. ;o)

Notes from ITY-Inputters

"Weener! Congrats on emptying your brain!" – C.B.

"Loved it. BTW, I think your brain-flush theory is a good one. Sleep is the time for the brain to renew and maybe pooping out the waste is part of that process." – T.L.

"A terrific article! SO good, in my opinion that I posted the link to the article to my FB page. Thanks for putting pen to paper (as it were) every so often. Cheers." – G.L.

"Trina, what a great outlook on life. Half way through or less I knew who the Farmers were (in this article). You have a great talent, so keep on writing. I have put your column in my bookmarks so I can read more of your articles." – J.L.

"I just read your column on sneezing; found it SO relatable! Yes, I've tried not closing my eyes – it is impossible. My father was a just-let-it-out sneezer; my mom made the attempt to stuff it inside. I used to tell her the same thing you wrote: that her head would explode. My warning went unheeded, but her head remained safe. For me, sneezing brings with it, as you said, a sense of satisfaction. So, I'll continue per usual. Thanks again for your unique viewpoint." – P.P.

"You do not know me. I have been meaning to write you for some time. I have enjoyed reading your columns. You are a strong woman with a lot of common sense and a wicked sense of humor. We live in Minden, having moved from Kansas five years ago, rural, farming background and can relate to much of what you write." – J.A.

"Enjoy reading your articles and always look forward to the next one. Keep them coming please and thanks for the chuckles!" – P.H.

"Hi Trina, Oh my gosh... You're just like chatting with a good gal pal when I read your awesome columns. You reference stuff just like I do. *Thanks* for being so real... I'm just a country farm girl from Minnesota but have lived everywhere including Mexico City, L.A., and... Phoenix etc. Sorry you lost your life partner (husband) recently. Hang in there. You *sound* a-ok so far... One day at a time... This too shall pass. Yes, like you say, 'This is me too.' Kindly God bless. Luv ya." – L.W.

"Well, howdy... Your stories sure pinpoint the fun fine brief moments in our lives that make one think with a smile. I can't say I have ever seen discombobulated in print before. I'll be darned." – D.M., Chicago

"I gotta tell you, this ITY is me all over again." – D.C., Idaho

"When I grow up, I want to be just like you, Trina!" – M.K.

"First of all, I admire your column because you do not immerse yourself in it. You only wet your feet in it. Like Mark Twain said, 'I take life seriously, but I take myself lightly.'" – D.G., Utah

"Well said, Trina, and congratulations on your success!" – A.M. a.k.a. B.M.

"Hi Trina, I just want to congratulate you on such an achievement. I've enjoyed all of your articles and look forward to them each week! I also want to wish you and husband a very merry Christmas and the best for the New Year!" – B.K., Carson City

Re: *My Nose Has Grown*
"Try: 'Cut off your nose *to spite* your face.' Make more sense? Love your columns!" – T.B.

"In your NV 'Appeal Memory Lane' column on November 23, 2019 first paragraph, you mentioned 'a sorted story.' Just curious, did you mean 'sorted' or 'sordid?' I enjoy your columns.

Re: *Don't Touch Me*
"Dear Ms. Machacek:
I mostly enjoyed your article this morning with the exception of your comment that the hippopotamus will drag its prey under water and eat it.
My dear, hippopotami are herbivores!
While they may bite one who appears to be a threat to their darling babies, I would be far more worried that they might step on me. Forgive my fussiness, however, it is the printing of such misinformation (or worse, gossip) that goes galloping around the world, becoming "fact" to the careless reader, who also fails to check for the accuracy of information. There, now I am finished. Do keep writing; you are clever and amusing. But, strive for truth!" – Your fan, W.S.

Re: *Have You Seen My Sunglasses?*
"I thought of that column last week when my reading glasses went missing on me. I'd put them on the ironing board so I would remember to take them with me when I left for the murder mystery rehearsal. But when I got to the rehearsal, I didn't have them with

me. Hmmm. Must still be on the ironing board. Except they weren't." – R.D.

Re: *Snack Master*

"I just had to let you know how much I enjoy your columns and how often I think, *we could be twins!* This latest about snacking is so dead on. I'm fairly good about them during the day, but once my (much-needed) sleep medication kicks in, all bets are off. Anyhow, I hope you continue to write for a long time." – T.P., Ely

Re: *Flu Shots*

"Trina, I read your column weekly in our local paper. Appreciate your perspectives – though we sometimes disagree. As you can guess, I take exception to your column last week on flu shots. Attached is a snarky piece written a few years back by a prominent infectious disease specialist; healthcare workers are his intended audience but I believe his advice is applicable to [the] general public as well. He gets carried away but makes some good points about the real value of flu vaccination – especially number three. Many of our long-term care residents are highly vulnerable to the disease, so visiting family and friends should do all they can to prevent spreading it. A flu shot is a simple first step, along with frequent hand washing and covering your mouth when sneezing. Looking forward to future columns! Thanks." – H.Q.

"I enjoyed your article today as I always do. I too struggled with the same issue with the dishwasher. I figured out the solution which is pretty common sense. I empty the bottom rack first so if anything on the top rack spills it doesn't get all over the clean dishes in the bottom rack. You're welcome!" – D.W.

They Call Me Weener!

(This last one says it all to me. This is exactly what I want to feel when I read stuff and so it's what I hope you feel when you read my words…T)

"Hey Trina, your article on septic tanks was a real classic. One thing about your 'stories' is, you can't wait to see what the next paragraph will be!" – Your fan, W.S.

Life is just such a hoot and a half!
Thanks for your time.
Happy, happy all the time,
Weener

Acknowledgments

As the time to publish this little book of mine got closer and closer, I nearly forgot to ask my wonderful editor, **Kara Scrivener of Emerging Ink Solutions** if I could do a thanks and acknowledgment page or two. Yes! She said yes! So…

Kara Scrivener of Emerging Ink Solutions is one grand editor and I can't thank her enough. From the note I got from her when she first read the title (she was laughing – always a good sign since this is a humor book) to edits, edits, edits, designing of the cover, and the zillions of questions I seem to always have, she never missed a beat. Even with a toddler at her feet! HAHA I did a ton of research before I let someone outside of my comfy circle get their hands on my baby and she stood out on so many spokes of a wheel. I highly recommend her. I hope we will continue to be partners in crime and friends. Even with all my Buts, HAHAs, and other things she tried to tell me were not needed or were too far out of the "norm." HAHA, you silly editor!

On this journey, my brother and sister-in-law Rod and Julie Russell picked me up whenever I fell and broke my crown. Rod loves to tell anyone who will listen that he taught me everything I know about writing… And I follow up with, "and thankfully I've forgotten all he ever said." Love ya, big brother! Julie is a beautiful woman who cooks better than I ever will and has enough love for me and her *huge* family. Love ya, sista! These two bundles of joy have always been my sis-boom-rah cheering squad to go, go, go as far as I can. All they ask for in return is Trina Tacos on Tuesdays when they come to visit. Easy peasy. Huggin' you two always.

How lucky am I to have a bunch of gal pals (and their husbands) who read my do-dahs and laugh with me? Some even find all the boo-boos I create because I think faster than I type. So to Carole (always up for an adventure) & Pete Bigrigg, Sue & Lynford Miller, Margaret & J.P. Kruckeberg, Pat Diehl, Sheryl Jackson, Leah Mendoza, Valencia "Goosey Margaret" Mitchell, Donna & Dennis Clark, Emma and John Sayler, Marcia (who hates the name Weener,

HEE-HEE) & Dale Elliott, Candy Castaneda, Karen Labarry, Leanna & Roland Good, Chicago Debbie Montgomery, and Nancy Peters – smooches to you all.

Two doctors I know have seen to it that my mind keeps going, have kept me on my stupid MS feet, and have promised to keep me going like nobody's business. My super hero neurologist Dr. Tim Louie and my wonderful neurosurgeon Dr. Jay Morgan – you guys are never out of my mind or my prayers. And just recently Nick Hirschi (APRN) and Tamisha Pena (ARPN) at our local medical clinic brought me through a patch that I don't think I would have come through without them being on my butt!

Who makes me happy? I never had children but since my happy-making other half Jerry zoomed to Heaven, I have been adopted as a mom by some wonderful "kids" in their 20s, 30s and very, very early 40s. *Wink, wink.* My kids from other mothers, HEE-HEE. They take care of me, chitty-chat with me, sit at my table with me, and laugh and cry with me. They have given me a wonderful gift. They push me to go, do, and be all while cheerleading me to get back into life and get this book done.

Who also makes me happy? Eleny Carrion, Jamie Pritchett, Mathew Bell, Kendra & Mike Zimmerman, Sam & Sheri Horst, and Zoe Ann Armknecht. I could just squish all your faces off!

Along this path I have acquired a few good-guy friends. I gotta tell ya, every girl needs guy pals who make them feel special. I hope I do the same for them. Thanks to my very best bud Lyn. Shout out to Dave Rhodes, Jimmy (wherever you have landed), Eddie Hennings, Dandy Randy Morgan, and Bob Klos – you guys are aces in my book. Literally!

Oh, and my heart of hearts, my ITY readers. To those who take time from their busy, busy days to read my words and send a note to say "HI!" To the new friends I have met in person, on Facebook, and Instagram. Wow! Thank you! Who knew, right? I am constantly learning who I am from such an amazing group of new and old friends. So very cool. Thanks!

To the editors, most of whom I have only met on the phone, of the newspaper that carry my column "Is This You?" weekly or occasionally. I remember trying to get Shellie Dutson, editor of the *Millard County Chronicle Progress* out of Delta, Utah to buy what I was selling. She finally plowed me on the phone one day – "You seem to always call on my busiest days when I am trying to go to print!" I was so embarrassed that I blubbered an apology and promised to only call on the day after press day. I called the next week and she *finally* said yes! She is one great gal and someone I have learned from. Always ask, "Is this a good time to talk?" On the whole, the editors I work with are hard-working men and women whom I will always be grateful to. I can't hardly wait to meet more just like them. Sell, sell, sell – HAHA!

I really didn't ever think I was a writer. I mean, come on. In my eyes, writers were these cool people with magical skills. Well Nancy McLelland, a writer, teacher, and great sandwich-maker who runs the Tuscarora Writers Retreat (which I highly recommend) in fabulous downtown Tuscarora, Nevada, was the one who, after a week-end session with her, finally sat me down and said I was indeed a writer. She taught me to close my eyes and feel my way through my backyard. That gave me perspective to "show instead of tell" in my writing. A wonderful talent I now use all the time. Thanks, Nancy, for your words, time, and a rousing kickstart in my butt. Makers Mark on the rocks on me soon, okay? Oh, and I can tell you that being a writer is a blessing from Him. It's kinda like magic, only better!

Finally, this one. I was popping through my e-mail one day and got a funny note from Carolyn Fox, a lady who was attending a seminar in Winnemucca, Nevada. That 30-plus-years-old annual seminar is a wonderful program called *Shooting the West* which brings wonderful professional (her) and newbie (aka me) photographers from all over the world together to teach and learn and just have such good times. *Yikers!* What good times! Carolyn read "Is This You?" in a newspaper she picked up at the Winnemucca airport while there on a photography class during *Shooting the West* in 2017. She wrote to tell me she laughed and from that one note we became grand friends.

She has me hooked on picture taking and we write real hand-written letters all year and chitty chatty at the doings in Winnemucca once a year now. Because I live in the dry arid desert, she treats me to wonderful oranges from her Duck Bar Ranch orchard and sends notes, funnies, and goodies all the time. She has also become someone I trust to tell me yea or nay of my writings, photography (such as it is), and any wild ideas that pop to the surface of my mind. She is a keeper and I can never repay her kindness and friendship. So, Carolyn, know this, you're a pitless peach in my bowl of life… You are sweet all the way through and I am blessed to have you in my circle!

You know that saying, "It takes a community to raise a child?" Well, my community has helped raise me from some dark depths and create this baby of a book. So, hey community! Thanks will never be enough. But it is heartfelt and my love runs deeper all the time, so bring your galoshes when you next come over because ya'll know "it" can get pretty deep at my house. HAHAHA.

Trust God to get you through and, of course, be
Happy, Happy All the Time!   ;o)
T

About the Author

Trina came into the world in Reno, Nevada in 1955, exactly six months between Christmases on June 25 – and it was snowing! In the late 60s, her family moved to the tiny town of Ely, Nevada where she went to high school, graduating in 1973. Trina's writing career began in her formative years but was put on the back-burner for the next 40-plus years until she bulldozed herself into her local newspaper in 2012 with her dream column "Is This You?"

Since that first column, a tiny voice has screamed at her to write, to complete the book you are holding. This book has been on Trina's to-do list for eons. It was something she really, *really* wanted.

Trina now lives in Eureka, Nevada where she has been for nearly 45 years. Her "other half" Jerry left this world in January of 2018 after 42 years of marriage. He had spent nearly 20 years burdened with illness and had been in need of constant home care for his final ten. Since then, Trina has focused on living – writing more, doing the things she only dreamt of doing during those wedded years, and honoring her life as Jerry's wife. Trina doesn't have many regrets except letting all those years go by without being able to write about them.

The future holds only new experiences. Trina recently went skydiving for her 65th birthday! She is constantly encouraged by her circle of grand friends that pull and push her when her feet stumble.

She often sings of how blessed she is to have been gifted with the talent of writing but very rarely knows how a story will end. She chalks her talent up to her faith; her talent is God's way of telling her she is alive. Truly, Trina is one person who is – happy, happy all the time.

Made in the USA
Columbia, SC
05 September 2020